Essentials of Fire Department
Customer Service

Fire Protection Publications
Oklahoma State University
Stillwater, OK 74078-8045

Alan V. Brunacini

RECYCLABLE

Copyright © 1996 by Alan V. Brunacini

ISBN 0-87939-127-8
Library of Congress 96-83497

First Edition
First Printing, February, 1996
Second Printing, February 1997
Third Printing, January 1998
Fourth Printing, 1999
Fifth Printing, April 2002
Sixth Printing, July 2005
Seventh Printing, January 2008
Eighth Printing, September 2011

10   9

Printed in the United States of America

Introduction
Essentials Of
Fire Department
Customer Service

This little manual is the result of a series of thoughts, ideas, hallucinations, and reflections relating to fire department customer service and is structured around the following opportunity categories:

1. Our essential mission and number one priority is to deliver the best possible service to our customers.

2. Always be nice — treat everyone with respect, kindness, patience, and consideration.

3. Always attempt to execute a standard problem-solving outcome: quick/effective/skillful/safe/caring/managed.

4. Regard everyone as a customer.

5. Consider how you and what you are doing looks to others.

6. Don't disqualify the customer with your qualifications.

7. Basic organizational behavior must become customer-centered.

8. We must continually improve our customer service performance.

Preface

You pay a visit to your friendly local library. You find your way to the "tell me what's ever been written about a particular subject" section. You sit down in front of a blank screen and enter FIRE DEPARTMENT CUSTOMER SERVICE. You bravely hit the "search" button. The machine springs to life. You hear the clutch clutching, the whirley-gig whirling....the supercharger kicks in....the lights dim in the building, the machine sputters and shakes, the screen flickers, lights up, and shows: "No such subject." You become anxious and bewildered. You obviously require a clinical intervention. A sofa visit to your shrink clearly indicates you should develop a hobby and stop asking dumb machines dumb questions. You begin to macrame athletic supporters for "B" shifters. Your stress vanishes. Life is good.

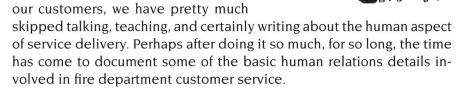

This lack of documentation about what seems should be a fairly major topic is a curious reality for an occupation that has been intensely and continuously serving customers for the past 200 years. Most firefighters come from the factory with a strong action orientation and a natural inclination to focus more on the "hard" technical-tactical part of the job, rather than on the "soft" human stuff. That may explain why, up until now, even though we basically have done a good job with our customers, we have pretty much skipped talking, teaching, and certainly writing about the human aspect of service delivery. Perhaps after doing it so much, for so long, the time has come to document some of the basic human relations details involved in fire department customer service.

At any rate, one day a while back, while we were sitting around polishing the silver, I started jotting down (those damned 3x5 cards again) some real simple customer service ideas and observations. As I kept doodling, I ended up organizing my mental gymnastics around some major topics/areas of opportunity. I ended up with eight. These eight (topics) seem to make sense and have held up pretty well as I have used them as the basic structure for writing the material in this little booklet. Like most of my projects, this one started out in my shirt pocket and ended up in the somewhat longer form you are now reading.

It seems that our service just naturally evolves through stages of development. Over the past two decades, we have discovered, implemented, and internalized significant improvements in the service we deliver. The equipment, software, and hardware we use to deliver those services is more advanced and most importantly of all, we have made major investments in increasing the skill level, understanding, and overall capability of our human resources —our firefighters. These efforts all add up to a package of improvements in our overall effectiveness that, taken together, produce a snapshot of our current stage of development.

human resources = our firefighters

Perhaps customer service becomes the next logical area we must take on in our on-going developmental process. Who knows — improving how we relate to the internal and external humans in our world may become the whipped cream and cherry on top of all the other developments we have worked so hard to achieve up until now. Using customer service development to add the finishing touches to the current stage of our basic operational approach may also provide access to the insight and intelligence from those who receive our service (our customers) that will identify what should be next on our continuous improvement menu. No developmental process will just naturally surrender information easily, so we must listen critically and pay attention as we proceed to the next stage of our development. Simply, if you don't learn to read the map and listen to the natives as you go along, it's pretty easy to get lost and stay lost, or to not know where you are when you arrive where you are.

A new character shows up in this material — Mrs. Smith. She really is not new — actually she has been around as long as we have. It's just in the past we have never very effectively included her in our thoughts, planning, and operations in the special way that makes her our customer. She represents the regular, real live people who call us for help when something burns, or something hurts, or something breaks. A lot of both her immediate and her long-term future depends on how we respond to her call for help, and how we treat her during our time together. I believe she (the customer) should begin to play the central role in both our personal and professional (occupational) mentality and in our organizational service delivery game plan.

Necessarily, a lot of my own personal context and orientation shows up in how I have approached and developed this material. It is difficult (or impossible) to separate yourself from your own system. I have joyfully passed through all of the stages of a firefighter's career (and life) from birth to senility, all within the Phoenix Fire Department. We are a very active (125,000 alarms - 1995), metro, full-service, career fire department, in what has been and still is a rapidly growing, dynamic sunbelt city. Phoenix is now the seventh largest city (1,100,000 population/470 square miles) in the United States.

Phoenix has been, and still is, a very progressive, positive, and encouraging place to operate and deliver service. The customer service material that follows is the result of my direct involvement with the Phoenix Fire Department during my entire adult (?) life. The service delivery examples I use are all true stories that actually have occurred in Phoenix. My observations have emerged out of almost forty years of being actively involved with the smartest, most capable, open, nicest, nuttiest, best-natured workforce on the planet. Our department members have been enormously patient with a steady stream of ideas, projects, experiments, and efforts that have produced the change required to continually "fix" our system (and us), and to move forward.

For the past twenty years, Phoenix firefighters have eaten change for breakfast and had fun doing it. I personally have received the best possible care and feeding a Fire Chief could humanly receive. I pinch myself (and smirk) at least twenty-five times a day for somehow landing in such a positive place, inhabited by such nice people.

The purpose of my shameless bragging (other than just shameless bragging) is to make a deal with the readers to first understand where I come from, and then to plug where they come from into the "Phoenix" material as they read it. Fire Departments are alike in a lot of ways, but we are also different in many other ways. In places and ways where we are similar, it's possible to bring new outside stuff in, plop it down in our system, and make it work pretty easily. The fun begins when we stumble onto a positive new idea that would improve the performance of our system, but conditions where it is working are different from us. This is where it's necessary to remodel, retool, re-engineer, or re-smush (sometimes completely disguise) the idea so that it effectively fits into your system. I guess customizing new stuff to somehow fit into our own system is a major part of the agony and ecstacy of the change and improvement process — and one of the big-time functions we pay leaders on every level to lead.

I have used this little booklet as a place to record (actually unload) a lot of stuff that I have been watching and thinking about for awhile. Some of it probably involves using our physical and human resources in some ways that may be a little outside the context (paradigm) of traditional fire service management and operations. Don't worry too much if reading it causes you to break out in big, itchy hives. It's only our typical reaction when someone or something smacks our comfort zone. The hives will go away in just a second and are probably reflective of the way most of us fire service managers have been raised. I can relate to this process because I (also) spend a lot of time recovering from "sticker shock" when one of my very secure (brilliant) 1972 perceptions/beliefs gets blasted with some lunatic 1996 reality.

The reader will probably deal with the material in a smorgasbord kind of way — take what tastes good and leave the rest. I hope that "tasting" the material breaks loose some new ideas on how we all can do an even better job for Mrs. Smith.

This material may find its way into the hands of nonfire service (that is, normal) people who have some interest in customer service. They must (simply) substitute their own job/business/occupation into any place they read firefighter, fire department, etc. I strongly suspect that basic, positive customer service is fairly universal and that while good fire department service is delivered in a bit more urgent way, it's not that different from driving a cab, flipping (and serving) pancakes, checking in sleepy hotel guests, or providing medical services to anxious hospital customers.

The reader will find this material to be simple, basic, and uncomplicated. It is not written in a very fancy or formal way. This approach is in no way meant to trivialize how much skill, effort, practice, and determination is required to deliver effective fire department customer service. What our troops face in the street can be enormously complex. A ton of books have been written (thankfully) about the detailed techniques we use to get the technical-tactical part of the job done. What might be different about this simple little essay is that it is meant only to describe the service delivery process from the position and feeling of the person who is receiving the service — our customer.

I have tried to write this like we were sitting around the fire station telling war stories and talking to each other. (I can't write well enough to disguise how I talk....you won't need a dictionary to understand the material.) The style and language is directed to those who work in the street to deliver service to real live customers so that they stay real and live.

My principal focus, orientation, and interest continues to be in the business end of our business where fire companies and customers come together. I have noticed that over the long haul in that exciting setting (the street), we are the most effective when we stick with the simple, basic stuff. I don't hang out with many academic or theoretical people (nice folks, but they talk funny), so it would be pretty tough for me to write any other way.

A lot of really smart people have reviewed this material. Most have observed that I must have received a somewhat better grade in Fire Fighting 101 than I did in English 101. I appreciate very much their patience in reading my ravings and improving the quality of the content without removing the street context. I also thank "Pooney" Pickering for dressing up my routine blab with his excellent illustrations. Pooney is both an experienced Phoenix Firefighter Paramedic and an excellent artist. Kathi Hilmes and Kevin Roche have both cheerfully packaged and repackaged the words as I have continued to reflect and scribble. They work hard every day trying to get me through the day and simply make life a joy for an old guy who gets lost a lot.

I also thank my old pal Doug Forsman and his Oklahoma State gang for their usual kindness and support. It's always nice to hang out with the very special people and place where you got started (OSU Class of '60).

As always, the author is ultimately responsible for any errors, omissions, goofs, or stuff that makes no sense.

I hope you have as much fun reading it as I had writing it.

Alan V. Brunacini, 1996

Our essential mission and number one priority is to deliver the best possible service to our customers.

1

Our essential mission and number one priority is to deliver the best possible service to our customers.

Today in the fire service, it's pretty easy to get distracted and lose track of why we are in business. Based on the possibility of us losing our way, it can be useful for us to look back at the very beginning of our service to see why we are what we are. It all started with a smart alec named Ben Franklin, who thought up a lot of answers to problems of his day. As ol' Ben hung out and watched the local color, he quickly identified that in those days there wasn't any organized community response when an unfriendly fire would visit a citizen. The typical outcome was that the fire would wreck everything and everybody that could not get out of its way. Ben basically invented the American Fire Service, as we know it today, to respond to the urgent needs of our ancestors who were threatened by fire.

Ben Franklin — invented the American Fire Service.

What he started then is pretty much still in place now. Based on the urgency of a fire event, he recognized that short response time capability is always a big deal, so he designed a highly decentralized system with fire stations located throughout the community. He recruited highly action-oriented, intrepid firefighters, who were (and still are) attracted to the excitement of responding to emergency episodes. He formed fire companies who instantly developed pride in their unit, responsibility for their first-due area, and became highly competitive (sometimes nuts) with each other. He connected the companies with a semi-military organization and command structure. He developed an alarm and dispatch system with quick and easy access.

The beauty of his fire fighting system was that it was very simple — when citizens (customers) had fires where they didn't want them, they contacted Ben and his merry band of fire extinguishers, who responded quickly and operated to evict the fire. They solved the problem and were nice to the citizens before, during, and after the fire. Ben's basic design set the stage for virtually all subsequent American fire service development and has produced a 200-year-old love affair between the fire service and our customers.

Predictably, since Ben's initial brainstorm, a lot of fire service change has occurred. Technology has shifted and we now use computers instead of bells, 8V92 diesel engines instead of human and horse-powered pullers and pumpers, SCBA instead of wet beards (!), and 8-watt portable radios instead of speaking trumpets. Current codes, standards, regulations, financial management (and mismanagement), labor and community relations, politics, instant electronic communications, liability, lots of lawyers, and every conceivable special interest group have also created a lot more complex operational and management setting (progress?).

Ben's original system design (decentralized/quick/action oriented) has also placed us in an ideal position to expand our service delivery menu to deliver other essential urgent services — emergency medical service, haz-mat, special operations, technical rescue, and an entire array of other community, social, and customer service responses. This service delivery expansion has now pretty much filled up our activity dance card.

It currently takes a big inventory of stuff and a bunch of various characters to provide the support required to effectively deliver service to our customers. It's pretty easy for that support to become separated and detached from the actual service delivery (to the customer) simply because the energy and effort of that support (inputs) typically occurs a long way from where and when the service (outputs) actually gets delivered. It becomes a heroic, ongoing organizational challenge to somehow keep the inputs and outputs connected. It takes an array of people, places, and things to package up Engine One to get out the door and show up at Mrs. Smith's kitchen fire. While the support workers are the ground crew that is required to get Engine One to effectively fly, they pretty much never get to take the trip themselves and deal directly with the ultimate part of the whole system — the customer on the street.

Throughout the organization there are behind-the-scene workers, like the admin guy who captures the bucks to buy a chain saw (a truck company favorite used for vertical ventilation and heavy-duty access operations), the clerk who types and processes the purchase order to buy the saw, the delivery kid who picks up broken saws and brings back fixed ones, and the guy who works all day in the back of the shop providing counseling and orthopedic services to wayward saws who have been ridden hard and put away wet.

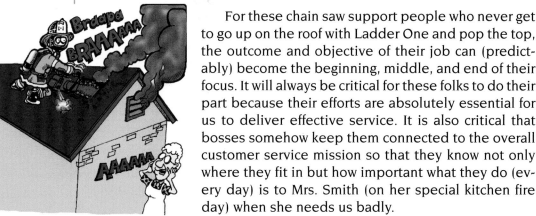

For these chain saw support people who never get to go up on the roof with Ladder One and pop the top, the outcome and objective of their job can (predictably) become the beginning, middle, and end of their focus. It will always be critical for these folks to do their part because their efforts are absolutely essential for us to deliver effective service. It is also critical that bosses somehow keep them connected to the overall customer service mission so that they know not only where they fit in but how important what they do (every day) is to Mrs. Smith (on her special kitchen fire day) when she needs us badly.

Note:

On the flip side of this process, the crew on Engine One had (also) better understand where they fit into the service delivery puzzle. They must approach their hero status with an appropriate amount of humility. It's pretty tough to act like Batman in a yellow helmet when the delivery guy and mechanic didn't show up, you have run out of Batbullets, and the Batmobile is so pooped from fighting evil that it won't fire up.

Mr. Smith is flying home from a business trip. He will change planes at the next stop to complete the journey. During the flight, he accidentally slips, falls, and injures his ankle. The flight crew stabilizes him, makes him as comfortable as they can, and radios ahead for a medical response team to be waiting at the gate. A paramedic engine company and an ambulance are dispatched to meet the plane. Upon landing, the medics quickly check Mr. Smith. He is stable with a painful ankle sprain.

They package him for a trip to the hospital for medical evaluation/treatment. The company officer makes arrangements with the gate agent to get Mr. Smith's luggage off the plane. This is done quickly and his bags are loaded with him in the ambulance. The officer also obtains the schedule for later departing flights to Mr. Smith's home destination and gets the agent's direct (double secret) phone number. The officer also gets Mr. Smith's home number and calls Mrs. Smith (at home) and explains what has happened. He describes what action is being taken and that Mr. Smith is essentially okay, but won't be chasing her (on foot at least) for a few days. The officer indicates (to Mrs. Smith) that Mr. Smith will be delayed, and he will call her later with details. Mr. Smith is transported to the closest hospital (3 miles). An emergency room doc shoots a couple of X-rays, stabilizes the ankle with a wrap, fixes him up with a crutch, and gives him two pain pills for the trip home. The hospital doc tells Mr. Smith to see his own doc when he gets home. The emergency room clerk gets the necessary insurance details and discharges him.

The ambulance crew has waited (in service and available) for Mr. Smith to get finished (hospital provides sandwiches/donuts in the lounge for the medics). During the treatment process, the crew has communicated with doc/nurses to estimate release time and has called the airline gate agent, who books Mr. Smith on the next flight home. Our ambulance delivers Mr. Smith back to the airport, checks his luggage, orders a wheelchair, and wheels him up to the counter to change his ticket. They say goodbye to Mr. Smith, wish him well, and tell him to lay off kicking field goals for several weeks. Airline personnel take over, get Mr. Smith to the gate, and the plane gets him home. The ambulance crew calls Mrs. Smith to give her arrival

flight details. In one week, Mr. Smith writes a letter to the Fire Chief (who didn't do anything), describes the service he received, and asks the Fire Chief to thank/commend the troops. The Fire Chief follows Mr. Smith's instructions.

What was the cost of the value the crew added to the service delivery event? First of all, they did a regular EMS sprained ankle intervention. This is the basic service that was delivered. Then, the company officer got Mr. Smith's bags (in case he had to spend the night), thought about getting him home after the hospital, and set it up with the gate agent. The ambo guys waited at the hospital (ate hospital chow and schmoozed with hospital types), and then drove Mr. Smith the three miles back to the airport. Nobody had to suffer a major (or minor) personality change. The crew independently solved the problem within their empowered organizational capability and resources, and added a big dose of nice. They treated Mr. (and Mrs.) Smith the way they would like to be treated if they landed in a strange place with a smushed ankle, and Bamo — WOW! service. This basic value-added approach uses our spirit and design as the basis for taking care of Mr. Smith.

While changes in technology, the current environment, our service delivery menu, and organizational complexity have created huge differences in our business, the most important element has not changed — the relationship and feeling between the customer who has a problem and the firefighter who responds to solve that problem. The two become intensely involved in a very special experience that defines essentially why we exist as a service. If we screw up that intense

relationship (for any reason), both the firefighter and the customer can be in big trouble. Ben set us up originally for the very simple, singular reason to deliver service to the person needing help; we basically and simply exist as an organization to respond to these urgent customer needs. Ben's original system design continues to send that timeless message in a very practical way. The most profound evidence of our existence to the customer is that we show up when they are having a bad day and call us for help. Based on that reality, being a firefighter involves making a promise to the customer that we will respond to their call and do our very best. If we become so modern, so distracted, or so overcome with our own qualifications and importance that we lose sight of that promise and can't get that vision back, we should make an adjustment in our fire service vocation/avocation and go sell aluminum siding to people who live in brick houses.

Handwritten margin notes:
Wow service — basic value added approach uses our spirit and design
2017 RA
most important element — relationship between the customer who has a problem & the FF who responds

Always be nice —
treat everyone with respect,
kindness, patience, and
consideration.

2.
Always be nice — treat everyone with respect, kindness, patience, and consideration.

To be effective, we must continually connect a lot of different organizational pieces into the operation of an integrated system. They include our physical assets (stuff) like facilities, equipment, tools, apparatus, electronics, SOPs, and software. Very little in our business is automated, so virtually all of these pieces require a real live human to make them operate. While these system components are absolutely essential to our operational effectiveness, they are in a special way "dumb" because they don't move very much or really do very much until a real live person comes along and hits the start button. Many times we become preoccupied with the mechanical, manipulative, technical, procedural, and tactical parts of our operation. While they are critical to our effective operation, they also require human activation. The point of this brilliant analysis is that while this part of our inventory is essential to deliver service to Mrs. Smith, it cannot by itself connect to her and with her as a customer. While she may admire the red and chrome and gold leaf, and may be impressed by the blinking/flashing light emitting  diodes, when the chips are down and she is in a bind, the hardware and software become transparent to the person in trouble who needs help. The only part of the system the customer will focus on, really care about, or remember very long is the human part of the system who directly delivers service and who touches them as a human in a human and caring way. Simply, it's difficult to really believe a digitized prerecorded electronic voice when it says it cares about you.

This human-to-human process begins with the initial call to request assistance. Mrs. Smith could care less that we have a space-age 911 electronic, nano-second, pass through computer driven call receipt and dispatch system with automatic address/phone verification capability and an instantaneous satellite-driven vehicle locator and an on-line computer terminal in the front seat of every vehicle that is painted red. Rather, she instantly connected with the voice and helpful feeling she received from a heads-up, calm, professional communications center

Critical initial
Stage —
dispatcher
Sent a
message
Help on the
way.

human. When Mrs. Smith sent the personal message that she was in trouble, the dispatcher sent a personal message back to her that the system cared about her and help was on the way — at that critical initial stage, the human (dispatcher) became the entire fire department to Mrs. Smith. As the event continues to evolve, Mrs. Smith somehow forgot to ask about the results of the last pump test on the rig that pulled up on Side A at her home. She will typically remember and relate (two page letter to the Fire Chief a week later) three basic observations about our service — none of it mentions pump test results (or anything else very technical):

#1 *Quick response time* — "It seemed you arrived as I was hanging up the phone."

#2 *Skillful performance that solved the problem* — "Your firefighters were so calm and took charge. Everything got better after they arrived."

#3 *Positive personal treatment* — "Everyone who responded was so kind, and I will never forget how nice they were to my family and to me."

Remember
and
Relate

2014

The most
important
and memorable part
of the fire service
delivery

Numbers 1 and 2 (QUICK/SKILLFUL) each get a nice three-sentence paragraph. Number 3 (NICE) gets a full page and a half from Mrs. Smith.

As Fire Department operational participants concerned with the long-term impact and effect of service to the customers within our community, we are absolutely compelled to examine the most consistently important and memorable part of the service delivery experience to the customer — being NICE. When we receive feedback, observe, review, critique, listen, and examine being nice within a fire department service delivery context, it involves the basic behaviors of respect, kindness, patience, and consideration. The service delivery expectation of these behaviors involves the following:

Respect:

- Introduce yourself to the customer. **

- Determine and use the customer's name that respectfully and effectively fits their profile.

- Listen carefully to understand the customer's position, perspective, and needs.

- Give the customer your exclusive attention.

- Develop solutions in terms of the customer's context and orientation — don't impose your values on the customer — ask them what is important.

- Operate within the customer's rights and privileges — become the customer's advocate.

- Be careful of what you say and how you say it — practice verbal etiquette.

- Deliver service, not bureaucratic regulations, to the customers — be honest.

- Quickly return control to the customers and move to "reconnect" their lives.

- Say thank-you.

Key Respect Words:
esteem, deference, friendship, affection, trust, honesty

Kindness:

- Use a positive, friendly tone of voice and body language.

- Use supportive and encouraging language that the customer understands.

- Indicate you understand and care about the customer's position and problem (empathy).

- Reflect professional concern and guide the customer through the problem-solving process.

[handwritten margin notes: use their name; Service Delivery expectation — Respect, Kindness, Patience, Consideration; become the customers advocate; Care = Understand & empathy; (thru kindness)]

** Time and the nature of the emergency are factors in the establishment of a relationship with your customer — introductions and resumé exchanges in the front yard of a burning house are not expected, taking the time to introduce yourself after the immediate emergency has passed is effective, expected, and nice.

- Be courteous and polite — be a sweetheart.
- Be gentle with the customer.
- Ask the customer about their needs.
- Try to keep the customer connected to their security symbols (items); a blankey and a bear is always good therapy.
- Try to make the customer as comfortable as possible.

Key Kindness Words:
   benevolence, humanity, generosity, charity, sympathy, compassion, tenderness

Patience:

- Take whatever time is required to establish positive interpersonal contact/communications with the customer.
- Explain what has happened, what you are doing, and what you think the outcome will be in clear, plain language.
- Work efficiently and explain the process and progress as you go.
- Spend extra time with the customer/family.
- Patiently attempt to "slow down," control, and stabilize the concern, fear, uneasiness of the customer — your calmness becomes contagious.
- Don't use excessively technical language — take the time to communicate in customer terms.

Key Patience Words:
   quiet perseverance, even-tempered care, composure, stability, calm fortitude, resilient courage in trying circumstances (that's a beautiful phrase)

Consideration:

- Quickly connect with the customer's profile.
- Whenever possible, ask the customer how you can construct a response to fit their needs — ask them where it hurts; ask them what is important to them; ask them what will make them feel better.
- As quickly as possible, return control to the customer and "unvictimize" them.
- Consider and respond to the needs of everyone involved in the incident (including Good Samaritans).
- Avoid value judgments that reflect your personal perspective/opinion.
- Design and extend the service in your professional terms — deliver the service in customer's terms and context.
- Be careful of the customer's property and possessions.

Key Considerate Words:
   showing kind awareness, regard for another's feelings and circumstances, thoughtful/sympathetic regard

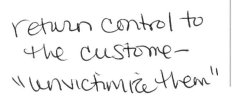

return control to the custome — "unvictimize them"

Mr. Smith is driving home in his car. He is a diabetic and his chemical-physiological balance goes haywire. He becomes disoriented and hits a curb, which stops his car and flattens one front tire. A neighbor (to his accident) sees his curb-crashing stop, recognizes he is having some physical difficulty, and calls us for check welfare-medical assistance. Our communications center dispatches a paramedic engine company (closest unit) and an ambulance. Our engine responds and arrives in three and a half minutes. Our members quickly establish contact with Mr. Smith, introduce themselves, and listen carefully to his situation status report. The team does a standard Advanced Life Support (ALS) assessment. They treat, stabilize, and package Mr. Smith for transportation. They explain their actions throughout the treatment process. The ambulance then transports Mr. Smith to the closest appropriate hospital.

dispatch - critical initial stage

A crew member establishes contact with the neighbor who made the original call for our help, describes in general terms what has occurred, the action we have taken, and thanks them for calling. We leave our standard department information packet with the caller. The company officer contacts Mrs. Smith on the Engine's cellular phone, indicates that her husband has had a minor mishap and is basically stable/okay. He tells her that the car is driveable and if she will get ready, the crew will pick her up and drive her to the hospital. Part of the crew changes the tire and then drives the car to the hospital. Other crew members drive to the Smith home (on their rig) and brief Mrs. Smith, secure the home (lights, stove, pets, locks) and then drive Mrs. Smith to the hospital where they accompany Mrs. Smith to the emergency room. At that point, we collect our EMS tools and our medics and our units go back into service and return to quarters.

WOW

The response to this event describes a practical, doable (in this case, actual) set of activities that are added to a regular service delivery event that creates a WOW! level of NICE. In this case, the basis of solving the customer's problem is the fast, effective delivery of ALS service — after that, we can begin to add value with NICE humane treatment that goes beyond standard emergency medical treatment.

Nice — combination of: high level technical skills delivery activity. definitive set of ways we humanely deliver service.

Nice isn't some blue sky, smiley-face program — it is a combination of both a definitive set of high level technical service delivery activities combined with another definitive set of ways we humanely deliver that service. While it may be just another day at the office for us, it's a pretty special day for the Smiths. It's hard to imagine any way that we could have handled the Smith's special day any better — just ask the Smiths.

Note:

This particular event occurred in a way that allowed the crew to add some important extra service and support beyond the effective delivery of a basic service: they were able to quickly reach Mrs. Smith on the phone; it was easy and fast to change the tire; and was manageable to drive by and pick up Mrs. Smith. Obviously, if the car was seriously crunched, it would have been towed off to the fix-up place. If Mrs. Smith was exploring the North Pole, the hospital or Mr. Smith would have contacted her and so on.

In any case, we have the chance to add value by first providing quick/effective customer-centered service and then going beyond that level to meet our definition of nice (WOW! level). This creates in and of itself an exceptional customer experience. Sometimes the situation (like this one) offers the opportunity to do some extra nice stuff that is outside our traditional approach (and mentality). These are the activities and experiences that over the long haul create an exceptional feeling, trust level, and loyalty among the customers, and a very special fire department reputation within the community.

This added value is the result of smart/capable fire crews that are empowered on their level to identify and respond to service delivery opportunities right on the spot and then being positively reinforced by bosses (also smart capable and empowered) who create an organizational experience and trust-based feeling that makes those crews want to do it again. Simply, we repeat behavior that is rewarded....pretty basic, huh?

Emotional Labor

The application of nice as a standard customer service characteristic adds an interesting new performance requirement to our business. We must deliver service (out in the real world) to a wide variety of customers and situations. Sometimes it's easy and natural to be nice. The customer is sane, lucid, oriented, and has a problem that is solvable within our regular system with our regular resources. In these positive situations, we like the customer, and we approve of their problem. On the other end of the scale, we find customers and problems that produce the opposite reaction (in us). These customers appear to be (and many times really are) nuts, disoriented, chemically scrambled, and generally unbalanced. Many times they have self-induced problems that

are the result of being dumb, irresponsible, mean, violent, and generally awful. Lots of these situations involve people who do not look, act, think, smell(!), talk, or behave like us. Delivering service in these difficult situations to such hapless souls (very unlike us) requires both physical effort and emotional labor.

This is where our "nice quotient" abruptly collides with reality — talking nice is easy, doing nice is tough. It's a piece of cake to rent a hall and have an "excellence" retreat (pep rally) that produces happy face slogans, buttons, and bumper stickers. The rubber abruptly meets the road when E1 gets a call at 2:30 a.m. (simply because there isn't anyone else to call), and they are nice to a deranged customer with a 65-year-old body and a 7-year-old mind, who is soaking wet, nude, locked inside a bathroom, hiding from aliens, that the crew is trying to coax out so they can check his or her physical welfare and then coordinate a ride to a rubber room at the funny farm.

When we encounter these tough events (and people), we must put on our nice game face and then orchestrate a standard service delivery performance. In the real world, this very simply involves acting — we don't feel nice, we may not really want to be nice, we may really want to choke the customer, but we simply act nice. This is where our job involves emotional labor. The application of this discipline and approach over time develops a natural and habitual capability and reaction to be nice in such tough situations — constantly nice behaviors produce consistently nice attitudes. This emotional labor must be supported by a strong service delivery game plan, a coordinated fire company team with a designated adult, and disciplined, patient players with the aptitude to do such difficult work.

In addition, we realize that our contact with the customer is typically episodic, short term, and we don't have to adopt them or take them home with us. The typical fast service delivery turnaround time creates a survivable customer service exposure when firefighters encounter tough people/situations. Our closed cab rigs also give us the capability for private stress relief after a particularly difficult encounter. We can engage in such sophisticated techniques as nerf batting each other, B-shift yoga, scream therapy, colorful oaths, or vulgar tantrums (below the audio level of the rig stereo). These highly "mature" techniques generally restore normal biorhythms and prepare us for the next high-quality service delivery opportunity. Team members who always play nice in not nice situations become the customer service role models and the authentic, quiet,

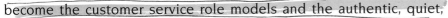
Always be nice — treat everyone with respect, kindness, patience, and consideration.

day-to-day heroes of our system — there should be a statue in every park in America (a great country) that recognizes the importance of their little (and big) acts of everyday humanity and kindness in difficult situations.

Always attempt to execute
a standard problem-solving
outcome: quick/effective/
skillful/safe/caring/managed.

3.

Always attempt to execute a standard problem-solving outcome: quick/effective/skillful/safe/caring/managed.

Intervention – Simple & primitive reason we are in business.

Our service is typically deployed using a combination of human, hardware, and software components that provide the capability to respond and intervene while the customer's problem is actually occurring. Intervention is the very simple and primitive reason we are in business. The separate deployment parts of our system are packaged in an integrated response and operational system that is designed to meet the regular and special needs of our customers. While the parts are fairly standard and nonmysterious (firefighters, stations, rolling stock, SOPs), each local area has its own special conditions that will require a somewhat different combination of components that make up the profile of that response system.

Customers trust us as pros to manage the system and expect that we will provide the correct combination of system pieces required for effective operation. They also expect that we have the capability (and inclination) to put all the pieces together in a way that solves their problem when they call us for help. Our current vision for effective service delivery involves coordinated teams of well-trained, managed, and motivated firefighters. These teams utilize the resources of the response system to deliver service in a way that delights(!) the customer.

Our goal – Create a WOW Reaction

The goal is to create a WOW! reaction in the person(s) receiving the service, watching the service being delivered, or hearing about the service after the event has concluded.

WOW! is the natural, involuntary, intense human reaction when receiving a service that is delivered in a way that is significantly, surprisingly, and positively beyond normal expectations.

Taking on a WOW! service delivery objective sends the strong message to everyone in the organization that the team is going to go way beyond "okay" and "all right" outcomes to consistently create a service delivery experience that exceeds what the customer expected or even imagined.

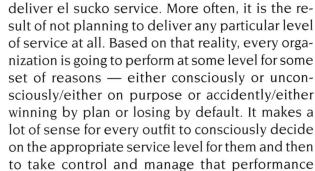

Service organizations perform at every level from lousy to WOW! In most cases, lousy performance is not the result of actually planning to deliver el sucko service. More often, it is the result of not planning to deliver any particular level of service at all. Based on that reality, every organization is going to perform at some level for some set of reasons — either consciously or unconsciously/either on purpose or accidentally/either winning by plan or losing by default. It makes a lot of sense for every outfit to consciously decide on the appropriate service level for them and then to take control and manage that performance level. Consistently excellent fire department service is the result of an explicit, long-term, planned, acted out, and refined organizational approach. The smart money will always bet on the future of any organization after watching how they regularly and consistently connect with their internal and external customers — this even applies to a group of fire service monopolists like us (big surprise).

It seems fairly clear that WOW! service produces nice outcomes like:

- Secures and maintains adequate resources and benefits.

- Happy customers, bosses, voters, and workers.

- Brings out the best in us — provides positive job satisfaction.

- Places us in the best position to compete (current challenge).

- Completes our basic customer promise.

- It's fun to be good and to do good.

- Doing it right the first time eliminates bad press, liability, lawyers, lots of meetings, and extra paperwork.

- It saves lives and lots of stuff that is really important to our customers.

- It's the right thing to do.

Delivering a WOW! level of service is a lot easier to say (and write about) than to actually pull off — particularly for an organization that must do what a fire department does, where and when we have to do it. We deliver service in the toughest situations to customers that are having days worse than bad.

Simply jumping on Big Red and going out to Mrs. Smith's kitchen fire ain't tiddlywinks. We pull off WOW! service with smart, tough, nice firefighters who think, pay attention, and play according to the WOW! game plan. Some of the plan is fairly detailed, some is pretty general and requires that we invent/improvise/adapt as we go.

Customers and their problems don't come with an instruction manual, so long-term, excellent service performance is the result of a refined system where empowered firefighters operate as much between the lines as they do on the line. This WOW! outcome requires that we describe and define how the service delivery execution process will occur. The parts that make up the operational plan become the very practical game plan of how we will deliver service to the customer at show time. Making such a service delivery plan consistently work is a big deal. It requires strong planning, continual practice, smart application, and refinement forever — this approach is the only way we can really get good and stay good. Delivering service in the street is always teaching us lessons (if we pay attention), so this

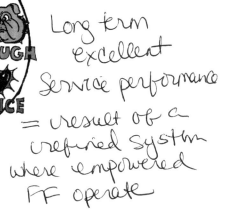

Long term excellent Service performance = result of a refined System where empowered FF operate

the plan - What
excellent service
will look like before
the event

the process - looks
like while its
going on

the outcome -
what it looks
like when its
over

approach is always under construction and is never complete. The service delivery plan gives us the capability to understand and then focus on what excellent service will look like before the event (the plan); what it will look like while it's going on (the process); and what it will look like after it's over (the outcome). The following are some of the major behaviors of an effective service delivery game plan:

- Quick
- Effective
- Skillful
- Safe
- Caring
- Managed

Quick

A major operational objective for our business is to arrive in time to interrupt the customer's problem while it's still in progress and interruptible. Maintaining this intervention response time capability is the entry price we must pay to get into the emergency service game — simply, if it ain't quick, it ain't emergency service and nothing else can make it so. A standard 911 customer expectation is that everyone and every part of the system will behave like the problem is an urgent event from the time we know about it until it's over. The process of reacting and performing quickly becomes a critical deployment objective throughout the incident. This is a major difference between being a firefighter and pumping gas and wiping windshields down at the Speedy Fill.

Effective

The other basic entry element we must come up with to get into and stay in the game is the very practical capability to consistently operate and perform in a manner that solves the incident problem. Speed and effectiveness form a critical partnership for us and the customer. Arriving quickly and being unable to perform puts us in the position to witness the event, not intervene in it. When this occurs, we are, in effect, dispatching inept spectators to the incident. The foundation of any level of service is effective execution that solves the problem. For fire department service delivery, added value (WOW!) can only occur after quick response and effective performance show up.

Skillful

Effective fire service delivery is mostly done by hand, up close and personal, by real live firefighters who work directly to solve the customer's problem. Such work requires a high degree of personal skill, integrated teamwork, and command coordination. A lot of apparatus, tools, and equipment typically are involved in our work, but it all requires human activation. The biggest, baddest fire trucks and the fanciest tools in town don't mean beans if our humanoids can't operate them.

There aren't many camouflaged engine companies or ninja firefighters, so most of our work is very observable and done in public view. Even customers without much experience can identify poor performers and poor performance. Flubbed work wrecks both the customer's stuff (for Mrs. Smith) and the customer's confidence in us (for Mrs. Smith, her neighbors, friends, and anyone passing by). We must manage and maintain a human performance management system that consistently prepares, supports, coaches, reinforces, rewards, and improves WOW! skill levels in our firefighters. *Simply, it is impossible for our system to outperform the skill level of our members.*

Safe

Firefighters must routinely work in hazardous areas to deliver service to customers whose bodies and stuff are being held hostage by a fire or other threats. We generally must get really close to the problem to solve it, and we can't control the setting where it occurs. If we could install handrails and a nonskid floor in Mrs. Smith's kitchen before she had a fire so that our firefighters would not slip and fall, we would also sprinkler her house so that when she leaves her pot on the stove a single head would open and zap the fire so that all we would have to do is chock a sprinkler and vacuum some water. Nothing will distract, disrupt, or derail our focus on delivering service any quicker than having a firefighter beat up, stuck, or missing. Simply, we can't do much about concluding Mrs. Smith's burning kitchen event while a paramedic is doing handstands on our chest, splinting our broken gazoo, or cooling our burned wazoo because we didn't protect ourselves or we did something really stupid.

We must capture the pieces of a response/operational safety and survival program and then consistently apply those components so that we can do our jobs in tough spots to solve the problem without becoming part of it. The customers expect us to protect ourselves so that we can go about the business of protecting them.

Caring

A fire department (or any other service organization) is a combination of two closely connected people games. The games involve the interplay between inside people and outside people. We call the inside people (us) firefighters — the outside people customers. The main reason the community maintains our inside response ability is to deliver service to the outside people who typically call us to solve urgent,

Inside people — us
Outside people — customers

mostly hazard-caused problems. How the service gets delivered on the outside becomes a direct reflection of how the insiders are cared for within the organization. The organizational context of care closely resembles that of a fire service family. This context becomes important because when we deliver service it is pretty much always a family deal. Emergency problems occur to humans and their stuff in a way that is most always connected to a family. Very few of the folks who need our help are absolute Lone Ranger characters who are completely by themselves — in fact, those who are Lone Ranger types have being alone on the list of problems we are presented with when we connect with them. Fires and other emergencies occur in structures that are family homes and in business buildings that are owned by families and that support families. Virtually every response contact involves our fire service family helping a customer family. This reality sets up the interesting dynamic that the understanding, kindness, and support we receive (or don't receive) inside of our own family automatically becomes the basis of the treatment we extend to our customers. Like any other family, we are made up of the standard family elements — incumbents, roles, relationships, ranks, values, politics, ancestors, history, and culture. We have parents, kids, uncles, aunts, grandparents, and godparents (don't screw with them) — kids grow up to be parents, parents become grandparents. We have family rituals, funerals, reunions, feuds, gossip, and family stories — we grieve when a family member is injured or dies. We have family favorites, family outcasts, sheep of all colors, prodigal sons (and daughters), family nuts, and anointed ones. We create and control by extending rewards and administering discipline.

The family process makes us insiders and causes us as insiders (firefighters) to feel and act a certain way about the customers, the family, and ourselves. We have the capacity and opportunity to be both enormously kind and supportive or cruel and monstrously mean to other family members — when the family (department) gets wrecked, it almost always occurs from the inside, not the outside.

Family/Organization wrecking process occurs when members — lose the feeling of ownership

The family/organization wrecking process occurs when members lose the feeling of ownership for their department. When this occurs, they begin to blame others on the outside for our own breakdowns and difficulties. Leaders on every level should be alert for the universal signal of this process — excessive reference to "they." When this happens, we become tenants who inhabit an organization that no longer belongs to us. We (simply) lose interest in taking care of it (nobody ever cared for a rental car the way they did their own cream puff '72 Chevy pickup). Blaming everyone (and everything) else for our problems is dysfunctional, lame, and distracts us from the reality that we are the short-, medium-, and long-term owners and custodians of our department (family). We define our own personal and professional present and future by how we take care of ourselves, each other, and the customers.

A critical outcome of being a member of a family is how you act when you leave home; for us, this is when we go out in the street to deliver service to the customer. If the fire department family is out of balance at home, there is a high probability that the service delivery event will be out of balance with the customer.... the current word to describe such screwed up families is dysfunctional. It becomes believable to deliver WOW! service on the outside if we receive WOW! care on the inside. Conversely, it's pretty illogical (actually goofy) for dysfunctional, abusing parents to drill the kids at home (dreary, unhappy place) to be nice to the neighbors' kids when they go out to play.

A negative internal organizational environment sets up a particularly difficult situation for firefighters who come from the factory naturally programmed to deliver good customer service and support. When these firefighters find themselves in a negative occupational situation, they (firefighters) become stuck between receiving lousy support and leadership on the inside, and being highly motivated to deliver just the opposite on the outside. Simply, it's tough over the long haul not to give back what you get. This produces a stress inducing bind that, over time, makes us personally and occupationally nuts. This is when the little light behind the eyes that lights the way to consistently doing the right thing goes dim, and we lose the heart and soul of our organization.

It's still pretty tough within our tall, skinny, vertical, old time, military model (system and mentality) to be overtly rude or revolutionary to your Jurassic Park monster boss. The longer the negative stuff goes on, the higher the possibility that we take out our frustrations at Mrs. Smith's kitchen fire. This is when and where we grab a Halligan Tool and the windows, interior finish, and pictures of little Billy on the coffee table substitute and take the hit for T-Rex Boss. The purpose of this little blivet of nickel psychology is not to justify frustrated firefighters becoming wrecking crews when they see their boss's scowling face in every piece of plate glass. It is only meant to describe both a reality that sadly still occurs in our business and the need to fix the problem where it actually occurs (family) and not where it pops out (Mrs. Smith's). The characteristic of caring becomes a defining event in our organization and directly effects how service will be delivered at show time. Like any family, the most critical dynamic and model of organizational caring is delivered by parents (bosses) to the kids (firefighters). This relationship produces independent, empowered, committed team member firefighters who get in between the customer and the problem and don't give up when things get tough. Good bosses create a level of tough love that eliminates negative, weak-kneed, drop-out, bed-wetting snivelers who lean and never lift. Bosses create and maintain what happens inside the organization. They must also support workers that deal directly with the customer during critical service delivery situations. Bosses take responsibility themselves, expand authority in others, and set the stage for either good or bad.... follow mean kids home and you find mean parents.

The fire service family has another interesting and unique profile that complicates the process of us caring for each other. Firefighters are tough people who many times must do dangerous, dirty, demanding work to protect the customers and their stuff. How this work (combat) occurs becomes the very real backdrop of our day-to-day environment. Effective performance and successful survival within this environment requires our members to be aggressive, inner directed, ready, and able to fight.(!) This active, energetic firefighter profile is very functional and necessary when we must overcome (i.e., fight) episodic, fast-moving, hazardous situations. The same set of characteristics can produce difficult interpersonal relations within the family in a way that is fairly predictable and pretty simple. During nonresponse times (which is most of the time) when we are not expending our energy on a fire or other physical problem, it is fairly natural for us to look around for some other energy-absorbing substitute. Many times we select our brothers and sisters as such a substitute "shock absorber".... they are close, convenient, and familiar. When this occurs, we simply don't have a fire to beat up so we beat up each other (interpersonally).

Historically, we have just expected and accepted this internal interaction as a normal and regular part of having a bunch of active, aggressive gladiators hanging around waiting to respond to the next unruly lion. Over time, how the gladiators treat each other becomes an important part of our ongoing culture. As young, entering firefighters live through being on the receiving end of the interpersonal abuse process (as a regular part of the organizational entry ritual), it becomes a normal expectation that such treatment just "comes with the job." Hope(?) for the future occurs when such young members, who are on the receiving end, realize that when they get additional seniority they can look forward to moving from the receiving end to the dishing-out side of the abuse festival. At that point (more seniority), the former recipients get to extend what they lived through to the next wave of entering members. As this process continues over time, it becomes genetically inevitable that we not only eat our young, but that we also create a goofy set of interpersonal reactions that many times we must live with for the remainder of that person's career.

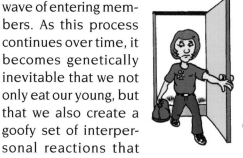

Currently, the custodians of the personnel, legal, human relations, and public opinion system outside the fire service have put a new spin on this old-time practice. These outside folks have redefined some of our lovable traditional behaviors. The contemporary terms "harassment" and "hostile workplace" have grown out of this redefinition and are now common new words that have jumped into our regular vocabulary. Abusive interpersonal behavior that in the past would have been described as just stupid sport is now defined, if it occurs in certain ways, as ranging from politically incorrect to clearly illegal. Teasing, joking, pranking, and jesting naturally occur (a lot) in our service. Where that interaction relates to gender, age, race, ethnicity, physical characteristics, rank, assignment, experience (or lack of), personality profile, shortness (particularly vicious), or any and all other personal differences can now be in the foul zone if that treatment puts the individual on the receiving end at a disadvantage. Another part of the new deal is that the recipient (not the donor) gets to define what is (and what is not) funny and what is damaging to them personally.

The basic problem begins with our inability to order firefighters from central casting with a split-personality switch. If such a model was available, we could flip the switch in one position and produce an attack-trained, conditioned, and inclined worker who would be preprogrammed to aggressively and effectively maim and kill fire and actively solve any other physical problem. For routine, nonemergency times, like when the kids are sitting around the station watching educational TV and eating Waldorf salad, we could flip the switch in the other direction and get a sensitive, emoting, considerate individual who naturally and positively relates to his/her coworkers (and everyone else). What happens in the real world is that we get a complete, connected, unswitched person, who as a firefighter is typically highly inclined and ready (thankfully) to do the tough business of our business. We quickly fall into the profile of being a firefighter and become a reflection of that work (adrenaline directed, intense, lots of camaraderie, always different, exciting); simply, if you work in the street you become the street. Our challenge is to creatively combine the somewhat opposite sets of characteristics represented by the two sides of the switch to get the most out of both sets of very necessary inclinations and capabilities.

Our current internal relations vision must reflect a basic change that eliminates these damaging (and now in some cases illegal) traditional fire service interpersonal behaviors. The versatility and intelligence of our firefighters (who actually have a lot of switches) make this change highly possible. The adjustment must begin with organization leaders on every level establishing new, modern guidelines that describe that dysfunctional interpersonal behavior as clearly unacceptable. Everyone must be trained and given a chance to understand (in a new sense) how such behavior damages the human resources and spirit of the organization. This is the most important reason for us to change. When we injure each other, that damage lasts virtually forever. Every firefighter can remember, with painful clarity, situations where their feelings were hurt by coworkers — in some cases, 30-40 years earlier. Generally, those who hurt their feelings were people they looked up to, and many were individuals the harmed person expected (by virtue of their rank, seniority, or stature) would protect them. Another important reason we should change involves what can happen to our department if we don't control ourselves. Many fire organizations where such harassment has not been managed internally are now being operated by someone in a black robe (ugghh). These are not happy places to come to work. Officers must do whatever is required to adjust behaviors in cases where harassment and abuse occur.

The message must be very simple: If you engage in harassment, you cannot be part of our organization — period(.).

Harassment creates a self-imposed organizational limitation that we simply can't outperform. There is no way to mush harassment around and somehow make it okay. The only effective response is to eliminate it. Self-discipline is by far the best control. If the "selves" can't control it, then the bosses must. If the bosses can't control it, the Department of Justice will. The objective of eliminating harassment is to remove the damage and distraction that it creates so that we can go beyond breaking even and get into the WOW! zone.

Eliminating harassment (very simply) improves the effectiveness of our human resources. This adjustment does not require we drop-kick the baby out of the tub — in fact, just the opposite. The absolute last thing the author (widely known as major fire service goof) would ever suggest is that we eliminate the teasing, joking, pranking, and jesting that goes on in our business. Removing that humor would wreck the soul of our service and would deprive us of the major capability we have to survive personally and organizationally. The author has always been at a distinct and happy disadvantage to appear as a stern disciplinarian because he is generally laughing at the latest humorous performance by some seriously and beautifully disturbed Phoenix firefighter. What now must occur is that we eliminate the hard, mean, ugly part of the junk that hurts us and leave the rest. By controlling ourselves in such a way, we bulletproof the safety of our internal environment so that we can get on with our own high-class, really funny, and sophisticated interpersonal relations.

The following are some basic observations about harassment:

- It always hurts us — inside and out.
- At some point, in some way, it will affect Mrs. Smith.
- If you have to ask (if it is harassment), simply don't do it.
- It's pretty easy to get out of balance.
- The receiver — not the sender — should decide if "the joke" is funny.
- Leaders must stop it — stopping it defines leaders (Big Time!).

- Some of the damage lasts forever.
- Don't ever approve of it.
- It's always expensive.
- If you did it — say you're sorry — don't do it anymore.
- Be nice.

Managed

Firefighters play the service delivery game a lot like a sports team — fast, complicated, action-oriented, exciting. There is a lot of sequential activity that occurs simultaneously within a compressed time frame. Both teams (sports/fire) utilize a regular starting point, strong standard roles, well-practiced plays, clear (primitive) performance targets, and effective leadership and coaching. Like a sports team, our best outcomes are fast and dirty. It is fairly easy for the participants and spectators to evaluate the action....simply, if you understand the game and pay attention, you can keep score.

Effective team management requires a coaching system that provides a plan for before, during, and after the event. SOPs and training establish and teach the plays before the game. SOPs provide both the basic plan while the game is going on and the review/revision component that evaluates how the players and plays performed. Local experience (how the game came out) is used as the basis to then reinforce and revise as required to help the system match the current local landscape. This "plan it," "do it," "review it" approach requires we package and manage the organization to learn, unlearn, and relearn quickly, because the local landscape is dynamic, complicated, sometimes dangerous, and is currently filled with many exciting, fast-moving opportunities.

– dept play book

The customer gets a clear message and impression from watching the team perform about how the team is managed and whether the event/response is under control. This impression becomes a major customer confidence factor. Everyone has stood in line for an hour, dealt with a rude worker, or had something that was still fouled up after you paid to have it fixed up and wondered who (and where) in the world is the fool who is supposed to be managing this mess. The basic management objective is to have our team win because of the coaching and not in spite of it. Good coaching is almost invisible to the customer — good service is enormously obvious.

Mr. Smith owns and operates a very active wood products (production) company that makes big-boy wood stuff — large wire spools, pallets, bracing, shoring, overseas packing crates, etc. His facility is in an urban industrial area. The whole complex occupies an entire city block and includes a large production structure (open shed), an office building, and what is (in effect) a lumber yard.

A major fire occurs at 1:30 a.m. in stacks of lumber. The fire also exposes and then involves the office building. We receive a 911 call and immediately dispatch a first-alarm structural fire response — 4 engines, 2 ladders, 1 medic, 1 command van, and 2 Battalion Chiefs. Our first-arriving company reports a deep-seated fire involving 100' x 150' of closely stacked lumber, plus the fire has extended to the interior of the well-involved 50' x 60' office building. The first officer assumes "Lumber Yard Command" (IC) and strikes a second alarm (4 more engines and 2 more ladders).

The IC begins to establish geographic operational sectors on all four sides of the fire. Their basic objective is to get in between what's burning and what is not burning to somehow keep it that way. The IC assigns arriving companies to the operating sectors who are basically engaged in a big-time, fast-and-dirty water fight, using large caliber ground and elevated master streams (surround and drown).

At the ten-minute elapsed time notification (from Alarm), the IC strikes a third alarm (another 4 engines and 2 ladders). At 30 minutes, all 12 engines and 6 ladders (plus support staff) are assigned, working, integrated into the incident action plan, and operating in a standard defensive manner. At 20 minutes into the event, off-duty officers who have been notified begin to arrive. They stage and become available for assignment. The IC assigns a Deputy Chief as the Owner-Occupant Support Sector Officer (O/O). The O/O calls Mr. Smith on his cellular phone, basically describes the situation, and asks him to respond. They establish a place where they will meet on the edge of the scene. When Mr. Smith arrives, the O/O meets him, gets him through the police line, takes him on a tour, describes the incident action plan, and they begin to discuss a recovery plan.

Mr. Smith indicates that the majority of his business is received from regular (repeat) customers over the telephone. The O/O indicates the office is basically toast and that all of Mr. Smith's telephones are now resting in AT&T heaven. The O/O contacts the fire department communications personnel (who actively deal with telephone people, places, and things). The commo guys wake up and begin to deal with Mr. Smith's telephone company (it's now 3:30 a.m.). The basic commo plan is to do whatever is required to cause the telephones to ring in a temporary office at 8:00 a.m.

The O/O calls Alarm and they begin to research and make contact with the closest motel to the scene to begin to coordinate and secure a place where Mr. Smith can set up a temporary office at the start of the business day (in 4 hours at 8:00 a.m.). Alarm makes a deal with the local Shady Rest Motel for two adjoining rooms. Resource Management (F.D.) moves folding tables and chairs into the temporary office. Our commo guys hook up cellular phones and coordinate switching over Mr. Smith's business numbers to ring at the Shady Rest.

Mr. Smith calls his supervisors and has them come to the incident site. They are briefed and discuss a plan to call workers at 6:00 a.m. to meet at the training room of the closest fire station to the scene (1 mile) at 7:00 a.m. This occurs — everyone is briefed and a basic plan is developed. The office workers go to the Shady Rest; the production crews go to the yard and begin to sort out what will be required to resume production — electric service, surviving lumber, damage to equipment, etc.

At 8:00 a.m., the phones start ringing at the Shady Rest. Customers are informed of the fire, orders are taken, and order takers extend the normal delivery time. Customers are understanding and wish everyone well. The O/O stays with Mr. Smith throughout most of the day and serves as the liaison between the fire event and the recovery plan. The O/O assists in renting and moving a portable office (two construction-type mobile home units) into the yard so that the temporary Shady Rest operation can move back home.

The next morning, fire department investigators move their mobile office (motor home) to the scene. They establish contact with Mr. Smith's insurance adjusters to begin to describe and document event details so that fire debris in the yard can begin to be cleared away and damage to the office can be evaluated. The fire department video unit shoots the entire scene (including overall God's-eye shots from a helicopter) to record a description of geography and damage. All video is made available to adjusters. Investigators remain on the scene

to continue to determine cause and origin and to assist adjusters. Both investigators and adjusters use the investigations mobile office facilities, phones, fax, etc. to create quicker recovery for Mr. Smith.

Let's use this event to compare the old fire-fighting-only days with the combined new-fire-fighting-and-customer-service approach. The author has attended (like most old firefighters) a lot of lumber yard fires. In the old days that's how they sold lumber — in old fashioned lumber yards. Today, it's all retailed in big, huge sales buildings by companies that have Club or Depot in their name. The buildings are glitzy, well-lit, sprinklered, and staffed by friendly "sales associates" in distinctive orange vests. In the old lumber yards, the guys who waited on you (?) were old carpenters with half their fingers missing. You had better speak carpenterese if you wanted to have a good day with them. The old lumber yards were big, fairly messy, and they generally had a beat-up old chain link fence around them. They typically had a lot of fires. When we had such a fire, we would call a mob of our colleagues, have a muster, and essentially put on a water festival. Generally, the owner would show up sometime during the fire fight (if he could get through the police line). He probably responded because some neighbor called him. We would sit him on the curb across the street and when either the fire or the water won, we would roll up the supply lines, say "so long" to Mr. Owner, and go home. In those days, our focus was on the fire fight and did not really include the customer. We were not being mean; it's just the way we did business.

Let's look at Mr. Smith's fire as an example of adding a customer service component to a regular fire fighting job:

- We conducted a standard old-time, low-tech, heavy-duty fire operation. We spoke to a big fire in the only language it will ever understand — big water. Jumbo stacks of burning stuff (like lumber) don't come gift wrapped for the fire department, so we had better be prepared to pump and apply lots of water. It has always been and will always be so.

- We designated someone (O/O) to deal directly with Mr. Smith early in the event. This is a regular part of our incident command structure. We had planned, organized, practiced, and refined it (O/O) before the event — all the IC had to do was to ID the need and assign it — Bamo, O/O is in business and dealing with Mr. Smith (the customer) — this requires a major change in our mentality and approach. In the old days, we treated the burning lumber like it was the customer. Now, the lumber comes with Mr. Smith who is the customer — not the other way around.

- The O/O called Mr. Smith, met him, gave him a tour and a briefing about what was going on. Mr. Smith received his exclusive attention. Together, they developed a plan for what to do next to keep Mr. Smith going. This approach creates a strong customer service beginning.

- The O/O did some standard recovery/support/assistance things to help Mr. Smith. He used regular fire department resources and capabilities to set up a temporary office and a way for the phones to ring. This got Mr. Smith up and operating with no business interruption.

- The O/O coordinated contacting Mr. Smith's employees, arranging a convenient meeting place, and assisted in briefing them on the situation. They had a chance to discuss and decide on a next step plan to keep the business going. This provided a lot more effective and sensible way to start on what was going to be a pretty confusing and traumatic day.

- Our investigators facilitated the front end of the adjustment process with the insurance company. The business was (obviously) seriously disrupted, and their support streamlined and shortened how quickly the initial recovery could begin.

All that adding a customer service element to a regular (old-time) operation cost us was a really minor amount of our people, resources, and time plus 3 dozen donuts and 4 pots of coffee for the meeting at our fire station with the workers. We started helping a fire customer before we had set up all the ladder pipes, and that planned customer assistance did not in any way slow down, interfere, or interrupt the pipes going up. Mr. Smith is a smart, capable businessman who would have figured out by himself everything he had to do to keep going in about

48 hours. It would have taken him this long only because this was his first (and hopefully last) fire event. We figured out and practiced what to do to help fire customers way before the fire occurred because Mr. Smith pays us to make that assistance and support our business....simply, he paid for WOW! service and he received that service.

Regard everyone
as a customer.

4.

Regard everyone as a customer.

It's pretty easy to develop tunnel vision when we deliver service because we are inclined to be highly preoccupied with and focused on the direct customer and their environment. While we should always give the customer our undivided attention (another item in this essay), we should realize that we are always on stage and that we are typically exposed to a lot of people.

A progressive change in our mentality (and approach) involves regarding everyone we encounter, both directly and indirectly, as a person who is our customer. This expanded customer consideration includes the person who receives our service directly and anyone who knows and is closely connected to that customer like family, neighbors, friends, or associates. This group generally has an intense interest, emotional connection, and personal concern for the welfare of the person receiving direct service and the effect and outcome of the emergency event. These people are very much an integral part of the incident, and we should treat them in a positive way and include them in our customer service incident action plan (respect, kindness, consideration, patience).

Family members are a very special group that many times require more attention than the main incident problem or customer. Family members become intensely involved, interested, and emotionally connected when a loved one is injured, sick, or threatened in any way. Situations that involve children or elderly relatives particularly require increased sensitivity on the part of our members. Many times the actual incident problem is very straightforward and solvable, but the reaction and involvement of family members requires another "treatment" focus and approach. Officers should include family members in their initial evaluation and develop an incident action plan for dealing with the entire family. The way we handle family members (either good or bad) creates a lasting memory and feeling.

As an example, every fire company has responded to a young mother whose kiddo fell down, bumped their head, and looked a little goofier than normal. She panics and calls 911 shrieking that little Throckmorton is having a cranial vapor lock. By the time we arrive the little devil is (thankfully) swinging from the chandeliers, but Mom is a basket case. The incident challenge then is to somehow calm her down while the kid is outside flipping toggle switches and blowing the air horn on the engine. What she will remember and what she will say once her brain waves

[handwritten margin note: A Group of people that many times require more attention than the main problem or customer = — family members.]

normalize is that she is embarrassed that she called us, but how nice (considerate/patient) the firefighters were to her personally. Such customers are not medical professionals (obviously) but they can recognize and will tell everyone they know what being treated by pros feels like.

The standard service delivery plan for effectively dealing with family members must include basic stuff like describing the situation, explaining our actions, determining their needs, and providing whatever service is needed to help them reconnect their lives. Developing an overall Department family support plan for how we will provide such services as making contact with family members, transporting family members as required to keep the family together, connecting with social, counseling, and support services and other community resources provides a strong ahead-of-time framework for fire companies to operate within. Simply, we must develop the resources and techniques to "treat" the entire scene, and family members are an integral and important part of that scene.

Many times the direct recipient of our service is in La La Land and will not remember anything about us except what their family tells them when they return to reality. In these situations, how we treat family members becomes the central focus of how we are remembered and how that family evaluates and relates the quality (basically, how nice we were) of our service. In these cases, the stories of how we delivered service to the Smiths becomes a part of that family's folklore and gets handed down to little Smiths as they hear the story re-told around the dinner table.

Another group we must consider is anyone close to the incident who is indirectly connected to the customer (who is receiving service) and the situation, like bystanders and spectators. This group typically does not know the direct customer. They watch what is going on and what we are doing because it is interesting and exciting to them. Their presence can be frustrating to us, particularly when they congest and obstruct the scene and our operations. We should develop, apply, and refine a plan to manage them in a positive way that gently moves them to a safe area and leaves a positive impression. The arrival of spectators should not be a big surprise to us — after all, we blasted everyone and everything within five miles with an enormous level of noise and blinking/flashing/strobing lights....not exactly a covert response.

Another group we should plan for and consider in our customer service game plan is the Good Samaritans who are somehow involved in and working on the incident problem before we arrive. These friendly helpers are typically giving aid and support to injured customers or those intrepid souls who have a garden hose on their neighbor's garage to keep the burning house from extending to Mrs. Smith's Nash Rambler. Many times they become part of the problem because they get to the incident early and, in some way, expose themselves to the incident hazard — simply, their motivation and good intentions can be way ahead of their safety training and survival procedures. Their hearts are always in the right place and the way we "take over" the event can either hurt their feelings or positively connect them to us and what we do next.

A real simple command/action transfer plan might include making positive contact with them (Good Sams), asking what has occurred and what action they have taken, and then listening to and acknowledging what they say. We should always check and verify their welfare (both physical and psychological). In some cases where these cooperatives are effectively (and safely) in place and doing good, let them continue to help us. It also makes sense to do a real simple, quick "credentials check" to find out who they are. It isn't real smart to blow off an orthopedic trauma surgeon so that we can deal with a broken leg (we really shouldn't blow off anyone). Another big (huge) deal is for us to simply thank them for what they have done. We should always secure the required details to record on incident reports and for a department citizen's award in positive situations. Imagine if we managed Good Samaritans in such a positive and encouraging way that we created an epidemic of people helping others in tough situations — what a WOW! outcome.

The motorists and pedestrians we meet responding to and returning from the incident create another (potentially large) group who we routinely encounter and who are a very critical part of the response process. These response neighbors are connected to us as captive spectators along the way who develop an impression about us and a reaction to us that is closely connected to our mutual safety and survival. We may expose ourselves to literally hundreds of people during our response to deliver service to a single person. Simply, how we drive our apparatus sends a message that we are either careful professionals or insane daredevils. We have high profile visibility wherever we go, and whatever we do attracts interest and attention during both routine and emergency times. Just the fact that we have shown up creates a certain amount of community disruption and commotion. Our apparatus is big, brightly colored, lit up, noisy, and many times we travel in a response mob. We make ourselves very obvious on purpose. The characteristics that cause people to notice us and get out of our way (hopefully) set the stage for widespread interest in us. Our presence indicates an event and intervention is underway, and normal people quickly recognize us and connect our presence with something at least potentially exciting going on.

This socialization starts early with kids playing with toy fire trucks that become a familiar and affectionate form/symbol to them. Most parents don't have the kid checked if he/she says at four years old that they want to become a firefighter when they grow up (some of us never outgrow that adolescent career plan.)

Other agencies

You don't have to wonder very long about what any other service business would give for our market position (besides us being a monopoly). Ask Pizza R' Us if they would like to have prepaid pizzas, a highly advertised three-digit phone number, legal permission to make deliveries code three with all warning devices blaring, blinking, and blasting (so your pistachio and tutti-frutti pie is always hot), and to have every kid in town playing with a toy pizza delivery truck from the time they can gurgle "Pepperoni and extra cheese, Mommy"....they want it, and we've got it!

An important group we must consider our customers are the other agencies we routinely deal with when we deliver service. They are folks like cops, EMS personnel (if we don't deliver the whole package), utilities, other city departments — like Streets, Traffic, Water, Public Works — doctors, nurses, and other hospital personnel.

We are closely connected to these people and their agencies and our relationship shifts based on the needs and details of each event. Sometimes we extend service to them and they are the customer. Other times we receive their service and we are the customer. Our willingness to customize our service to their needs when they are the customer gives us a practical opportunity to set the stage in a positive way for when we become customers and are on the receiving end.

It makes big sense to develop a relationship with them and a plan for how to effectively play together way before the game. Strong partnerships are the product of mutual inclusion in the entire program management package: developing interagency SOPs, training together, reserving a seat in the Command Post, conducting interagency critiques, sharing credit (and blame), along with continual revising and fine tuning based on experience and new info.

Every agency can do their job/specialty best. When we combine capability we all get stronger. Replace "I'm in charge here" with "What can I do to help?" Develop and practice strong relationships — not the reverse. You go first — rent the hall, send out the invitations, print an agenda, bring the donuts, listen a lot, take notes, clean up afterward, and then print and distribute the minutes. Pretty soon getting along and being nice becomes a habit.

Everyone in the community recognizes us, has at least some interest in what we do, and basically starts out (life) with the positive feeling that we are the friendly helpers you call when something hurts. We should regard our community profile as a unique opportunity. The clear message in this opportunity is not to disqualify anyone from being a customer candidate just because they are not a direct service recipient. We have the opportunity to consistently create a positive impression, feeling, perception, and memory wherever we are and with whomever we encounter. The starting point for us to expand our positive image is to use an inclusive customer definition as the foundation for developing a strategy to continually improve how we present ourselves in the community. We will discuss such a strategy in Section 5 which comes next....keep readin'.

Roscoe Smith (Mrs. S's uncle) and Jake go for a ride in their 1962 Studebaker. Roscoe is a 185-pound, 67-year-old retired steel worker. Jake is a 42-pound reformed car-chasing canine of mixed, but noble, parentage. Roscoe and Jake have been close associates since the very beginning of Jake's puppyhood.

As usual, Roscoe is driving and Jake is riding shotgun. They are both listening to Willy sing about his wasted youth on the AM. During their ride, an inattentive driver in a full-size sedan "busts" a stop sign and T-bones the old Studebaker in an intersection. The collision seriously injures Roscoe. Jake is shaken up but okay.

We receive a 911 call about the accident, dispatch an ALS engine, a ladder company for extrication, and an ambulance. Upon arrival, the engine Captain assumes command, quickly evaluates the situation, coordinates extrication, and assigns the medics to Roscoe. No one in the other car is injured. The Captain then introduces himself to Jake, establishes positive rapport, and identifies that the dog is basically uninjured and okay. The Captain has the crew put Jake in the cab of the engine and instructs the engineer to maintain an awareness of his security and welfare. Roscoe (who is still conscious) indicates to the medics he is very concerned about Jake.

They reassure him that the pooch is all right and not to worry — they will take care of him. After extrication, Roscoe is stabilized and packaged for transport. The medics and ambo crew then take him to the closest trauma center. The engine and ladder crews secure the scene and the engine Captain indicates to the police IC that he and his crew will transport Jake to the neighborhood veterinarian for an exam and boarding. The Captain calls ahead to the vet's office, gives them a brief description of what has happened, and makes Jake a reservation for a nonsmoking single with a view. The vet's office confirms the reservation and says to come ahead with Jake and they will be waiting for him. The Captain and the remaining crew members deliver Jake to the vet on the engine. The trip is approximately 1-1/2 miles. They check Jake in, give the office staff a description of the accident, and indicate Roscoe's hospital details. The crew also tells the staff how to contact them if they can assist Jake in any way.

The Captain has told the medics to call him before they leave the hospital. They do and the Captain gives them the

name, location, and phone number of the vet's office. The medics have the hospital staff include that information on Roscoe's medical records and ask them to reassure Roscoe that Jake is okay and being looked after by the vet. The next shift, the crew calls the vet's office to check on Jake. The vet indicates he is in good condition and is a very well-behaved guest. The engine and ambo routinely do business with the local trauma center where Roscoe is recovering. On their first (of many) trips to the facility on their next shift, they look in on Roscoe (who is recovering) to be certain he has received a status report on Jake. Roscoe is happy to see the crew and thanks them (profusely) for taking care of Jake. Roscoe proudly tells the crew Jake's life story from puppy to the present. The crew agrees that Jake is a noble specimen, says, "so long", and returns to the station.

In ten days, Roscoe is released from the hospital, able to get around and drive his backup Studebaker. On his first excursion, he picks up Jake at the vet's, visits the local doughnut shop, and takes a gigantic box of dough balls by the station. The crew is pleased to see them both and they all have a happy reunion. They (Roscoe and Jake) thank the crew again for their help and kindness, hop in the Studie, and drive away listening to the Hag grapple with the dilemma of whether the character he is singing about actually has a drinking problem or is just a man whose problems cause him to drink. Roscoe later writes a letter to the Fire Chief describing how the crew went above and beyond, directly to WOW! The Fire Chief prepares an exceptional performance unit citation that reinforces the department's policy of providing exceptional service to both human and animal customers and thanks them for being so nice.

Many of our customers (like Roscoe) have pets (like Jake) and they generally regard those pets as members of their family. Simply, these pets come along with the human customers and are a very important part of their lives. Every firefighter who has been around a while has had a customer say "my baby's still inside" to later discover the "baby" is a 15 year-old cat named Bartholomew.

The point of this pet essay is that we should develop a policy and the related procedures that describe the details of how we will handle and manage our customer's pets when they become involved in an emergency incident. The procedures should clearly state that firefighters should sensibly regulate the risks involved in rescuing pets (no power line, tree, or heavy fire rescues). The procedures should detail how we will secure and protect animals, how we will transport injured animals for treatment, and how we will respectfully manage dead animals. Such procedures could range from the department doing pet management themselves to having the local animal control agency or the humane society assist. Developing an ahead-of-time arrangement with the local veterinarian community to assist also makes sense. Vets are very typically really nice people who love animals, and most will assist and support fire department operations where pets are involved.

Consider how you and
what you are doing looks
to others.

5.
Consider how you and what you are doing looks to others.

As previously stated (over and over) every part of our system is firefighter driven and directed. This includes how we look to the customers — as individuals and as an organization.

This impression is created and maintained by the direct and indirect impression and feeling the customers develop in response to the appearance, performance, and behavior of our members. Simply, we create a human customer reaction in response to how our human firefighters look and what we are doing (human/human).

Our image must be planned and managed at the point and moment the customer impression is created. We never get that opportunity back — the deodorant ad says "you never get a second chance to make a first impression" (they ought to know).

The firefighter in control of that customer impression becomes, in effect, our department image maker. This creates the very practical reality that the really high impact of our customer contact system is the human part. This quickly shows that our firefighters are directly in control of the customer service delivery experience. It also shows that fire department managers have no real capability (and hopefully no inclination) to guard the customers from the firefighters.

If we examine the way we are organized and structured to deliver service, there is only one way we can effectively support our human resources (firefighters). That is to develop a simple customer service plan, to train our firefighters on the plan, and to depend on and trust them to directly execute the plan properly, where and when the customer service opportunity occurs.

The general objective of the positive image plan is to create the consistent customer observation and opinion that we are professional, under control, functionally focused, serious, effective, and friendly. When we show up, we should look like we are there to do business, like we know our business, and that we mean business.

The parts of a plan to create and maintain a positive department appearance and image include the following basic elements:

- Members
- Facilities

- Fire apparatus, tools, and equipment
- Presence/behavior

Members

Individual firefighter appearance creates an important first impression that becomes the unspoken introduction and beginning for the event. This includes the old-fashioned stuff like well-maintained uniforms, grooming, fitness, overall bearing, and stature. Having a fire department team show up all looking alike (that's why we call 'em uniforms), shaved, combed, standing tall, awake, and generally looking like they are serious is a pretty smart way to start doing business with the customer.

Our personal/organizational appearance should be part of a planned strategy to create a positive initial and ongoing customer impression and reaction. We don't have to wear epaulets and tuxedo pants to create that positive impression. Our customers are smart enough to know that what we do to solve their problem generally involves some amount of skillful manual labor — so we should try to look like smart, nice people who are dressed neatly; distinctively identified with both our name and our department colors; and ready to go to work. Once the event is underway, we don't get to trade anything for our appearance, but it "gets us in the door."

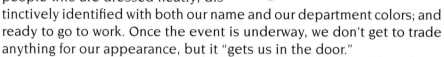

The basic objective is to create the long-term identity and feeling within the community that when a customer sees a uniformed firefighter, he/she is one of us, and they can trust that person to be in their bedroom at 3:00 a.m. to deliver medical services to their family and for them to know that it's really okay for us to have a lockbox key on the dash of Engine One that lets us into every bank in town.

While our uniforms reflect the individual and diverse history, tradition, style, and approach of each department, today (in the author's opinion) understated appearance is probably better than overstated. A nonmilitary/nonpolice appearing uniform may create a more positive and friendly reception and may be actually safer in the violent, nutty environment our troops must currently deliver service in.

Well-marked, distinctive tee shirts, golf shirts, and sweat shirts create a relaxed, professional look and feeling and clearly identifies us as firefighters, not police officers, airline pilots, or Italian marching band leaders. Such uniforms send more of a message that we are ready for action (like an athlete) rather than to control (like a police officer).

They lend themselves to silk screening our department name on the back so that every member becomes a mobile department billboard. "T-shirt management" is popular with our members based on being practical, comfortable, and sensible.

Uniforms are a big deal because they give us pride, identity, indicate a critical community function, and connect us to important department and fire service traditions. Showing up looking like the New York Yankees produces a lot different effect than showing up looking like a cross between a rock band and an itinerant carnival crew. A lot of times we act out how we look.

Facilities

The part of our organizational operetta where the fat lady starts singing is the scene where the firefighters and the customers come together. If you closely watch the show, you quickly see that customers are continuously surrounded by a complicated, many times mean-spirited, dangerous, and unpredictable environment. In addition to our human resources, we utilize a lot of facilities, apparatus, and mechanical/electronic stuff to effectively protect them when that complex environment jabs them, pokes them, falls on them, burns around them, captures them, or when the denizens of that environment get ugly with each other.

Short response time management requires we locate and house ourselves throughout the community in decentralized facilities that physically place us close to the customer (B. Franklin invention). This geographic dispersion game plan necessarily places fire stations inside the neighborhoods they protect. This location approach causes us to be an integral part and presence in that local place. Over time, Mrs. Smith becomes familiar and comfortable with "her fire station" located down on the corner. As she sees us actually living in "her" fire station, she develops a quiet confidence that we are close, we are easy to reach, and that we will respond quickly if she needs help because we are located right down the street.

Occupying a neighborhood fire station provides the customer easy access and an ongoing opportunity to view, evaluate, and develop a judgment of how well that facility is being operated. The fact that the station is a public building also gives that customer the right to make that judgment. We develop about the same set of relationships as any other neighbor and also are evaluated like any other family who lives down the block. The first (and easiest) way we will be evaluated will relate to the outside appearance of the station.

Our customers will naturally make a connection between how we will deliver service (to them as a customer) and how we take care of our house. This is not complicated or mysterious — we have all driven (hungrily) past a junky looking diner based on a concern that the same guy who takes care (?) of the outside of the joint might also be in charge of washing dishes and cleaning up the kitchen. Just like uniforms, we can't trade anything for a neat looking facility, but a positive appearance creates a nice introduction and sends the message that we are proud to be part of the hood. While we don't have to maintain a manicured, formal English garden out front, having a well-maintained station, with the yard squared away and the flag flying right side up, is a simple and practical indication that the lights are on and someone is home.

[handwritten margin note: physically place us close to the customer — decentralized facilities]

Fire Apparatus, Tools, and Equipment

Fire trucks are another dead give away that we are hanging around and doing business. Our apparatus is an important source of identity and pride and indicates our special customer service mission. Our rigs are very distinctive looking and decorated in highly symbolic and traditional ways. A well-designed and maintained fire machine inherently sends a positive, action-oriented message to the world that we are ready, willing, and able to hit the road and handle the customer's problem.

The way we maintain our apparatus is another indicator of how we feel about our mission. Watching a highly detailed piece of full-dress fire apparatus responding "under steam" (all warning devices activated) with a crew that looks like they are ready to go to work is truly a religious experience. Anyone not impressed with such a WOW! response spectacle is suffering a serious psychological/emotional deficit and should be quickly evaluated and given shock treatment. Fire trucks are Godlike vehicles that should always be overmaintained as a labor of love (personal and professional) so that they can protect good and fight evil.

Many times protecting the customer (and fighting evil) requires us to perform functions that involve tools and equipment. The tools of our trade are highly versatile and range from Frankenstein-like-primitive, manual, and mechanical forcible entry/access tools to highly sophisticated electronic medical equipment. When a particular tool is required to perform a particular function, it must be used quickly, skillfully, and under control.

The feedback loop of our work is painfully short — almost instantaneous — so if the firefighter can't make the tool work, or if the tool conks out, the operation generally stops, but the problem goes on. Anyone and everyone watching us operate will quickly identify if the tool/worker process was a hit or a miss. Our operations require (first) a steady stream of adequate, appropriate tool use that (second) produces a steady stream of completed work steps that integrate and move toward solving the overall incident problem.

Our tools are typically well designed/constructed, functional, rugged, action-oriented, high tech or very basic to match the job. They are very impressive. Watching skilled firefighters use such tools to extricate a trapped motorist customer or jump start a shorted-out medical customer isn't any different than watching a skilled carpenter construct a roof assembly or a snooty waiter deftly prepare a Caesar salad (with extra anchovies, please).

Presence/Behavior

The ecstasy (and sometimes agony) of being a firefighter is showing up in the morning, stashing your banana suit on Big Red, checking your mask, getting your first cup of starter fluid, and then taking on anything and everything that occurs in your franchise area during your watch. Some of the nonurgent activity can be scheduled during that tour by us, but the active (urgent) service delivery part is mostly scheduled by Mrs. Smith's emergency. Simply, we don't get to make an appointment with her to have her kitchen fire occur at a time that fits in between physical fitness and prefire planning.

The unscheduled, episodic characteristic of fire department work is a major attraction and a big reason why most of us psychos become firefighters. This reality makes being a firefighter a lot different than working down at the Tastee Freeze or the Ajax Manufacturing Company....both fine and essential organizations, just different (in that way) from us.

A major management challenge is how to construct practical, useful direction to help our troops maintain an effective appearance, stature, and the functional behaviors that consistently produce a positive appearance and impression as they go through their mix and match tour of duty. One way we use to create some of that direction involves the development and application of standard operating procedures (which has its own section later on). These procedures provide the organizational and operational basis (generally in some detail) for how we conduct business. They are designed to provide a common starting point and approach for executing standard operations in fairly standard situations. While they are very helpful in providing direction and to effectively connect the team, it would be virtually impossible to construct absolute guidelines for how firefighters conduct themselves to create a positive impression in every possible unstructured, nonstandard, and unusual situation they routinely become involved in.

SOP.

Based on the exciting backdrop of where, when, and how we do our work, probably the most useful approach is for the team to create and refine a set of basic, general image/impression ground rules. Leaders should then extend the support and trust to the troops to go out in the brave new world, to creatively apply those guidelines in between and on the lines (SOPs), and to have a nice day. (The author strongly suspects this approach lands somewhere close to the current popular notion of "empowerment.")

This approach seems to make a lot more sense than constructing 150 rules for where/how we can/can't, go/not go, do/not do and then spending the next 20 years frustrating everyone in the department trying to make sense out of understanding/applying/enforcing them.

The objective of this approach is to simply and naturally ask, "How does what I am doing look to Mrs. Smith?" by the firefighter who is in control of that activity right where and when it occurs. Mrs. Smith is a regular, normal person who looks at things in the community in a reasonable way. She is not the self-appointed, eccentric watchdog of government workers who follows us around with binoculars and a video camera to "catch us" doing something wrong. Every system seems to have such zealots, who should be treated gently, but it doesn't make much sense to develop an appearance standard to suit them because it would require we hide out in caves. In fact, we should encourage our troops to become a part of their neighborhood/community and to meet and get to know the customers before they need us in an emergency. This contact creates the opportunity to introduce ourselves, talk

about our services, explain how our customers can protect themselves, answer their questions, and give them a chance to see the quality of our personnel.

Our "behavior-in-public ground rules" should be realistic, functional, good-natured, and member centered. While we should always have a subtle, built-in tape running that asks how what we are doing looks, this should be a natural, nonstressful approach that doesn't make us so concerned that we develop a nervous tic. Firefighters are smart, nice people, and if they do what comes naturally, we are pretty close to being on track — all the tape does is help us stay inside the smart zone. Firefighters are a special part of the community and should be a familiar, positive, and active sight to the customers.

Protecting the people and property of the community is our job, and it requires we understand and have a knowledge of how our customers are situated. That familiarity requires we visit, draw, train, plan, discuss, practice, and reflect on the entire community. Simply, we can't have that knowledge and hide out in the fire station.

We also live in our neighborhood while we are on duty and must do about everything any other neighbor does to get through the day. We mow the lawn, wash the windows, clean the truck, conduct fitness activities, we relax (stand by), we eat (boy, do we), watch TV, visit/gossip, talk on the phone, and sometimes we sit on the front porch and watch the cars go by.

We also leave the fire station to do a lot of nonemergency, in-service activity in our first-due area. We do pre-incident building/area pre-planning, conduct training activities, do public education, do physical fitness, shop for groceries, participate in community events, and sometimes we stop and get a big gulp or a mocha rocky road almond praline ice cream cone.

This is all normal, regular, legitimate activity that creates the exposure and opportunity to look like pros or like buffoons. A set of guideline categories designed to create a positive public impression might include the following:

- Practice coordinated team management.
- Incident Etiquette.
- Wherever possible, follow SOPs/Mission Statement/Organizational Values.
- Avoid Unbusinesslike Impressions.
  - Right place — right time/wrong place — wrong time.
  - Hazard of excessive congregation.
  - Not joking in the wrong place.
  - Keep a clean workplace.
- Give the customer your undivided attention.
- Don't act like delivering service is an inconvenience to you.

Practice Coordinated Team Management

Watching us play quickly shows we are a lot more like a hockey team (in so many wonderful ways) than an individual figure skater. Virtually all the service we deliver is packaged and extended in teams of action-oriented firefighters. We play a position on some team from our first fire service day to our last. Just like the hockey team, our mentality is basically tactical (centers around problem solving) and involves the composition, formation, and deployment of our team, and the moves the team(s) make to execute operationally. An ongoing organizational objective is to standardize our team execution and match that standard execution (plays) to standard conditions and situations to produce standard outcomes....all this effective standardization blabbing attempts to connect playing with winning (prevent losing).

How the team performs at Mrs. Smith's creates a major part of not only the overall outcome, but the impression of us she develops. Effective team players complete standard roles and functions that fit together with the rest of the team to get the job done. Ideally, this occurs in a natural, quiet way that reflects planning, preparation, and practice. The initial team leader (generally company officer) becomes the identifiable (to Mrs. Smith) incident commander and coordinates his/her team efforts, evaluates conditions, and calls for the adequate and appropriate resources that will be required to deal with the entire situation, including Mrs. Smith, family, pets, neighbors, spectators, etc.

A major team coordination and integration element that Mrs. Smith (and everyone else) will notice is the interpersonal conduct inside and among the team(s). How the team deals with each other becomes a major indicator of how we are connected (or disconnected). If the team members are calm, polite, and considerate of each other and discuss, listen to each other, and decide on correct action, we look like we have a smart, together act. If we are rude to each other, if we yell at each other, if we disagree about what is correct action, if we argue and beat our chests about who is in charge, we look like big dopes.

In fact, how we treat each other becomes an important part of the service delivery experience regardless of how we treat Mrs. Smith — we send a screwy (mixed) message when we are nice to her and ugly with each other. She has to wonder if us being nice to her is an act or if we are truly schizophrenic.

Another indicator of how our team plays occurs when the IC escalates the response and more of us show up. How the later-arriving team members are integrated into the existing operation becomes a major signal of how we are connected. A smooth transition that increases our overall capability becomes an important indicator of not only the management of our system but also the relationships within it.

A very practical (and frequent) example of a smooth transition involves the initial and ongoing information management routine we go through with the customer. If the initial information status is passed on as more of us arrive, we appear effectively connected. If the customer must repeat the same complete status report over and over, including a

Effective team info

Planned
practiced ✗
refined procedures

complete description of their childhood including their mother's maiden name for each successive arriving responder, we look pretty detached and disconnected. Effective team-information management is always the result of planned, practiced, and refined procedures.

Delivering fire/medical service in the street can be a high energy, high stress, action-oriented process that occurs very quickly and many times in an emotionally charged setting. If we don't practice and play according to the team plan, it's pretty easy to get grumpy with each other. It's tough for Mrs. Smith to have much confidence in us controlling her problem — or a very positive memory of us at all — if we can't control ourselves.

Incident Etiquette

Incident operational service delivery is the most basic and essential reason we exist. The operations that deliver service to Mrs. Smith define us personally and create our department identity (if they don't, what does?). A major element in the incident operational process is how we treat each other during these rough and ready times. Simply, how Engine 3 deals with Engine 4 while they play together at show time creates a compelling and durable impression and reaction inside and outside our system (i.e. family) about how we regard each other. Incident operations are typically fast and dirty and there is generally enough running room within our SOPs to allow us to be inside of the boundaries of the technical and tactical guidelines and still treat each other a lot of different ways. Those ways range along the treatment scale from positive (nice) to negative (not so nice). The department's incident relationship standards among team members can create an overall (positive) expectation and should be explicitly stated, carefully evaluated, and critically managed by bosses on every level. Patrolling the perimeter around this interpersonal treatment (etiquette) becomes a major role for such bosses during incident operations. If the kids use the fast moving, many times unstructured, times that occur during fire fighting and other incident operations to be mean, ugly, or grumpy with each other, their parents (bosses) must quickly correct such behavior. Conversely, kids that play nice and help each other should be hugged and kissed. Like about everything else in our system, bosses must become and always be the role model examples of how being nice looks during tough times.

We continually plan, train, practice, discuss, simulate, and fantasize about show time, so being effective during these emergency operations is very important to us. Our incident operational capability is a major element in how we feel about our jobs, each other, and (most important) about ourselves. How our teammates treat us (as internal customers who are on the receiving end of the treatment process) when the most important part of our job is occurring, sends a high impact message that sticks with you. Being treated in a positive helpful way by your teammates when the chips are down creates a reinforcing connection among the team. This positive treatment causes the idea that we are truly internal customers to come to life and become very believable. When the opposite occurs and we use response events as a free-for-all to mug each other, we move the major challenge from solving the incident problem (like putting out the fire) to somehow surviving the negative interpersonal experience. Over time, such bad treatment results in firefighters (smart-adaptable) "hiding out" or working around the edges of the operation to avoid recurring negative interactions. We naturally attempt to avoid painful outcomes.

By nature, operating at fire/EMS/special ops events is tough. Firefighters expect (actually love) rough and tumble conditions where and when they do their jobs. We are highly durable people who must develop the ability to bounce back after the game — if we want to keep playing. We routinely yell, shout, shove, grab, and gesture to communicate, protect, direct, and manage each other — when we are chasing the fire or when the fire is chasing us (and the customer) and the falling roof is about to compress us into short midgets, we cannot do poetry and chamber music. This is the real world of our work and is not what this little "be nice" section is about. What this blab is directed toward involves team members being mean/ugly/inconsiderate to each other in a way that puts the recipient at a disadvantage while they are doing their job and makes them feel lousy after the event because of these negative experiences. It may well be that after Mrs. Smith's kitchen fire, she never deals directly with us again. The opposite is true of the team that operates at her event. We are permanently connected to each other. If E3 beats up E4 they are going to see them again (and again). Many times, the only chance (and the starting point) we have of controlling the problem is if we can control ourselves — we should include how we treat each other as an important part of that control.

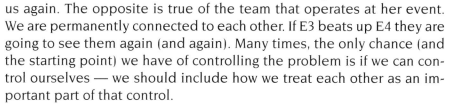

Virtually every situation we respond to requires the effective action of a team of firefighters. It is impossible for any team to move beyond how they treat each other and how they feel about each other. Interpersonal relations during high stress incident operations are an internal customer big deal. It is worth us developing the following list of some of the etiquette items that could be included in the curriculum of an incident operations charm school:

- Don't take advantage of the situation (or anything else).
- Don't hide in confusion.
- Everyone works for the IC — don't free lance.
- Respect the arrival order — use staging to stay in line.
- Decisions and actions should be driven by:
  - ❏ SOPs   ❏ Conscious Decision
  - ❏ Direct Order   ❏ Eliminate "deification occurs"
- Operate to best advantage within the plan and system.
- Assist and back up those who need help:
  - Young help the old (muscle and energy) — old accept that help.

- Old help the young (cunning and crafty experience) — young accept that help.
- Reflect a controlled hustle but don't race.
- Bring your positive attitude to the incident — leave your ego at home.
- If you must violate the plan, compensate and tell the IC.
- Everyone cannot be on the nozzle.
- Practice incident self-discipline.
    - Stay together.
    - Practice positive follower-ship.
    - Stay in your job/role.
    - Do your share of the mundane — dull stuff.
- Be a team player — make everyone look good.
- Make the person ahead of you safe and successful.
- Work hard to do your share, plus some/don't stand around when others are working.
- Manage incidents as non-political events:
    - Make assignments based on response/arrival order.
    - Don't play favorites.
    - Don't pay folks back for something they have done.
    - Equalize dirty/yucky jobs.
    - Share good/fun jobs.
    - Give credit where it belongs.
    - Coach and correct problems.
- If we are called by another agency, we deliver service to them and they are our customer — act like it.
- Operate to reduce (not create) incident stress.
- Expect and don't be surprised by:
    - Confusion.
    - Chaos.
    - Excited-emotional people.
    - Poor communications.
    - Compressed time frames.
- Operate safely — stay under control.
- Listen for orders, follow orders.
- Answer on the first radio call.
- Don't blab on the radio.
- Tell the IC the important stuff he/she can use.
- Tell the IC when you finish your task and are available — if you can't complete your task, say so.
- Talk nice to everyone — even when you're yelling (even when it hurts).

- When you ask, shut up and listen to the answer.

- Thank those who help you.

- Tell the truth — don't fib about task completion.

- Don't leave early — stay in the game until it's over.

- If you want to know what happened, ask. Don't make assumptions.

- After the event, talk nice about each other.

- Be loyal to the team, don't ever talk un-nice about each other (is un-nice a word?).

    .... Always be nice.

Whenever Possible, Follow Standard Operating Procedures/Mission Statement/Organizational Values

As previously stated, quick, effective performance is the basic entry price we must come up with to get into and stay in the good service game. Such positive tactical performance will consistently emerge out of us using SOPs as the basis of our operations. The SOP process involves the entire organization deciding on the most correct and best use of department resources on the strategic, tactical, and task levels.

Procedures become a powerful performance management element because they form the centerpiece foundation of a process that mobilizes and connects deciding/training/applying/reviewing before, during, and after the incident. Procedures are constantly reviewed and refined based on their application to actual service delivery experiences.

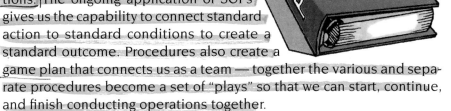

Procedures outline the way we will operate in a standard situation and how we will react to standard conditions. The ongoing application of SOPs gives us the capability to connect standard action to standard conditions to create a standard outcome. Procedures also create a game plan that connects us as a team — together the various and separate procedures become a set of "plays" so that we can start, continue, and finish conducting operations together.

This approach provides the best opportunity (and structure) to put actual local experiences "in the bank" so that we can become individually and collectively smarter; the last event is used to improve the next event. No single person or single part of the system can duplicate this organization-wide process and the energy it attracts to continually improve effectiveness.

Most tactical situations are a combination of a lot of standard elements and some special factors. SOPs become the operational foundation for sorting out and responding to the profile of each particular event — our standard approach becomes the starting point of our special approach. Effectively adapting to special, unusual, or different situations and conditions emerges out of standard operations. Equipping the team with SOPs going into the event creates a strong, standard beginning. We

(handwritten margin notes:)
Follow SOP.
Strategic
tactical
tasks

SOP - Play book
Procedures - game plan

use SOPs for the regular part of the incident. We then develop and apply customized responses for the special parts that are "left over." This makes it a lot easier than having to invent a plan for every part of the incident. Our standard approach provides the launching pad for us to creatively invent solutions as we go.

Our procedures become transparent to the customer. Simply, they don't know (or probably care) why we do what we do the way we do it, but they see the outcome pretty quickly, and they know what they see. Most of us don't know how to read music or understand the complicated sports plays (both SOPs), but we still enjoy the concert and/or the game. When our customer observes and remarks, "You make it look so easy and simple," they have generally watched (and been impressed with) the execution of a set of connected, coordinated SOPs.

Effective service delivery innovation and creativity consistently emerge out of us approaching SOPs as being expansive and not restrictive. They are in place and meant to provide the standard foundation and starting point for firefighters to develop whatever solutions are required to get the job done for the customer. SOPs are not in place to describe anywhere close to every situation that firefighters routinely encounter — much less the screwy, unusual stuff that occurs. Sometimes a routine event has some parts that are special. Sometimes the whole event is unusual and nonroutine. Effective incident management involves quickly sorting out the routine and special stuff. SOPs are not an excuse to limit yourself and what you can and will do for the customer. It makes zero sense for workers as smart, capable, and resourceful as firefighters to stand by and observe an urgent event evolve with digits in orifices because some part of the system straightjacketed them by not allowing them to take any action without complete SOP direction. Today, anybody in our business who must have an SOP for every situation before they can operate is seriously disabled and obsolete. In the 911 world of today, anything can and does happen. Each member of the team is responsible for using his or her brain to give input to solve the problem(s). Empowered firefighters along with their team members operating under the direction of strong, effective company officers who are guided by clearly stated organizational values, naturally and automatically take over wherever SOPs leave off. SOPs create the logical, practical, and very effective foundation and framework for us to act out our basic mission statement (values).

Many fire department mission statements are long and very flowery. Some sound a lot like an academy award acceptance speech. I always wonder how much of one of these Gettysburg Address operettas Engine One can actually remember at Mrs. Smith's at 3:00 a.m.

The mission statement I like the most is short (5 words) and sweet. It's so simple you don't have to write it down to remember it. It goes like this:

- Prevent Harm
- Survive
- Be Nice

The ongoing application of prevent harm/survive/be nice becomes the action-oriented foundation for our organizational "common sense." It makes our sense of who we are, what we do, and how we do it — COMMON. Simple, huh? Over time, leaders establish the mission and then support and reinforce workers who act out these mission objectives. This process causes the action that surrounds our customer mission to become the principal organizational focus. This positive service delivery focus gives us a fighting chance to displace the traditional, dysfunctional fire service "static" (power/control/rank/politics) that always negatively distracts a lot more than positively directs. In my travels, I hear a lot of us old geezers whine that today's young firefighters don't have any "common sense" (like we did?). This nongenetic deficiency may be a reflection that we brilliant old soldiers haven't effectively packaged up, taught, modeled, and reinforced the organizational goals, style, and objectives very effectively (or in some cases at all).

Prevent Harm

This statement very quickly describes why we are in business and creates the organizational direction and authorization to help the customers (people, animals, and things) we encounter who are in some way threatened, being harmed, or out of balance. We do this (manage harm) in a way that depends on when we enter the event. The very best approach is to prevent the harm before it happens. When harm is occurring, we must then respond in a way that interrupts and reduces that harm. Once the harm has occurred, we must help the customer recover in any way we can. This help typically is directed to those who call us or those we encounter within the general context of our overall fire department mission. Staying within that mission causes us to stick to what we do best — maintain an effective, ongoing focus on the kinds of routine and special problems that visit Mrs. Smith and how we can help her with those problems. This focus also prevents us from getting up some morning, having a big breakfast, and taking on global warming or world hunger (very legitimate problems....but not on our radar screen).

Survive

This one word part of the mission statement is easy to say — hard to do. Survive means to prepare, engage, endure, and recover from all the fire service occupational and personal bad stuff that can (simply) cause us not to survive. The organization acts out regarding members (us) as valuable internal customers in an enormously profound way by providing the resources (equipment, systems, support, love) to cause us to consistently and successfully survive what is a tough job on every level. The most un-nice thing that can happen inside our system is for one of our humans to get injured/killed. The exposure and possibility of this occurring comes along with the highly hazardous job of being a firefighter. How the organization protects their members from this most un-nice (injury/death) outcome becomes the very practical, heavy-duty message that forms the foundation of the organizational caring process. This important beginning occurs at the most believable (or unbelievable) and primitive level. This process occurs on the familiar old hierarchy of needs scale (Maslow). Getting your wazoo busted will always take you abruptly down to the survival level where it is pretty tough to worry a whole lot about self-actualization. Protecting our members requires we put our money, systems, and leadership where our mouth is. Making this investment on the bottom end provides the launching pad to get to the top end. It's pretty easy (and cheap) to say that our firefighters (human assets) are our most important resource. The way we physically protect those assets in the street will actually show if us saying this is real or baloney. No one will know the authenticity (or the opposite) of this "our firefighters are our most important asset" process any more than the firefighters themselves. They are on the up close and personal end of the occupational pain and pleasure process.

Historically, we worried about fire-damaged buildings falling on us (they still do). Today a lot of other things "fall on us." Based on that awareness, we are now taking a lot more holistic, long-term approach to supporting our members from both the episodic, abrupt survival challenges and also the longer term quality of life issues. All our ugly old enemies like driving accidents, structural collapse, thermal insult, and smoke exposure are alive and well and are still out there waiting to kick our butt. They are now joined by the new guys — infectious and toxic exposure; incident and organizational stress; life-style dysfunctions; and intense, incessant, and dehumanizing change. The timeless hazards beat us up and kill us in old-fashioned blue-collar ways. The new stuff beats us up and croaks us in modern color coordinated ways — the result is exactly the same — Keep it simple....be smart, pay attention, think, always follow the safety survival rules, and stick together — have a nice day.

Be "Nice"

essence of our whole customer service drill

This innocent, two-word, six-letter phrase within our mission statement becomes the essence of this whole customer service drill. Nice (one word by itself) is pretty easy to play games with — getting all the "nice" answers right, smiling, and nodding our heads at the right time, enthusiastically agreeing that "nice" is "nice," and singing the "nice national anthem," will probably get us an "A" in Nice-101. The class lets out and the games stop when we make it a two-word deal — be nice. The addition of BE makes it an action plan and requires we stop talking and actually crank up nice and take it out into the street. BE NICE is where the tread hits the pavement and becomes the tough part of acting nice out in the strange, exciting, cold, mean, violent, ugly, beautiful world of being a firefighter.

What this means as a big-time value (and mission) within our organization is to be nice to the customers, to each other, and to yourself. Be nice must become the most powerful and directive value we can create. It is our magnetic North....if you forget the SOP, if you are somewhat confused about just what is going on, if you don't know at that very moment exactly what to do, if you get separated from your copy of the straight-shooters bible — simply, *be nice and do nice*. The very best, simple, nonalgebraic (golden) test of nice is what treatment you would like if you were on the receiving end.

Frank Smith (Mrs. Smith's cousin) is an active, self-employed cement finisher. On a summer morning, he is

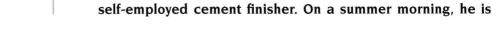

making a nine-yard pour. The job is an unremarkable and routine (flat rectangular) driveway — he has done hundreds of them before. Just as he completes his second pass with the bull float (big trowel with a long 10'-12' handle), he has a heart attack and collapses. A motorist passing by notices his problem and calls 911 on their cellular phone. We dispatch the closest paramedic engine company and an ambulance. Upon our arrival, the troops determine that Frank is indeed having a serious coronary event and immediately begin standard initial advanced life support treatment. They establish telemetry contact with their base station hospital. Their doc gives the orders required to complete the treatment and packaging process. At that point, Frank is loaded into the ambulance and, accompanied by a paramedic, he is transported to the receiving hospital.

The engine company Captain then surveys and evaluates the scene. He determines that Frank was well along but had not completed with the finishing job. He also determines that on this warm (90 degree) morning, the concrete is quickly setting up. He (typical firefighter) is familiar enough with concrete work to understand basically what's left to be done to save the concrete and the short time frame of that opportunity. He knows that concrete costs $60 a yard (times 9 or 10, he estimates), plus the preparation cost to excavate and form, plus the cost of finishing. He also realizes that a half-finished concrete driveway is pretty ugly, so if the job is not complete, it is essentially ruined. Then the unfinished (ugly) concrete must be jackhammered out, hauled away, and the whole installation and finishing process must start over. The Captain estimates (off the top of his head) a $2,500-$3,000 loss if the next (and final) finishing steps are not complete. He also realizes that his loss control window is quickly closing. A huddle among the crew indicates that two of the members of the adjacent ladder company which is first due to their location, do cement finishing on their days off duty. The Captain calls the ladder company officer on his cellular phone and tells him what's going on. The ladder officer asks his firefighters if they would be substitute finishers. They say, "Yes, and let's hurry."

At that point the ladder company responds, in service (available on the radio), to "concrete central." Upon their arrival, the two firefighter finishers go to work using Frank's tools. They make two-hand trowel passes and edge all around the driveway. This essentially completes the job that Frank started. The operation takes 30-40 minutes. Meanwhile, the engine Captain has called their Battalion Chief and asks him to respond to eliminate any surprises in case someone inquires why two fire trucks and a bunch of firefighters appear as if they have taken fire service productivity to a new and unusual level. The Battalion Chief (BC) and the two Captains observe the completion of the job. The troops clean up Frank's tools, load them into his pickup truck, drive the truck back, and secure it at the engine company's station. Back in quarters, the engine Captain calls the hospital and has them tell Frank's family that the pickup truck (and tools) are okay and secured at the station. He also asks them to let Frank know that the firefighter elves have finished the driveway job and to not worry about it.

That evening, the BC has the ladder respond to the engine's station, and he (BC) brings two gallons of pistachio-nut, tutti-fruity, chunky-monkey, fatty-daddy ice cream. The BC thanks both crews and indicates how proud he is of them all. They hang out long enough to enjoy the ice cream and tell some department war stories before the ladder and BC go home. The BC also completes unit citations of exceptional performance (green sheets) for both companies. When Frank recovers and is released from the hospital, he visits both the driveway job site and the fire station. He thanks the troops and compliments them on both their medical treatment capability and their cement finishing (he indicates they made it look better than he could). He says how happy (and surprised) he has been to find out what a full-service fire department he has protecting him (and his concrete).

This response is a good example of our members delivering service in an unusual situation based on the prevent harm/survive/be nice organizational values. They delivered our basic emergency medical service in a standard way based on standard procedures, that part of our response did not require very much (if any) special adaptation. We do that part of our job as a regular function all the time and our regular procedures cover it nicely. Beyond the regular medical service (a basic core business), our officer identified (based on perception, intelligence, and experience) a special set of circumstances that were not covered by regular SOPs. This is where our basic organizational values and the empowerment of our members kick in.

This situation and the response of our troops create an excellent example of how empowering firefighters actually works in the street — the concrete is setting up; if the final finishing steps are not done pretty soon, the driveway will be ruined. By the time the Captain could get a substitute finisher from the outside world, the concrete would be history. He uses on-line, quick-response department resources to get the right people, in the right place, at the right time, doing the correct action to save the folks we work for (the customers) from having to take a $2,000-$3,000 loss. The organization instructed us all to use our brains and imagination along with department resources to prevent harm, to be nice, and to not get beat up doing it. In the concrete finishing case, our troops modeled that mission, and their boss (BC) thanked and commended them for their action.

This approach is absolutely critical to us, because many times the problems we are involved in (like the concrete) have a shrinking window of opportunity that is very dynamic and perishable. If we screw around with big permission (CYA) festivals, the opportunity to do good simply goes away. For us, empowerment gives our troops permission ahead of time to episodically get us into a somewhat different activity beyond our regular, core business if our temporary entry into that somewhat different business will help a customer. After the event is over, we go back to minding our own business and looking for more opportunities to help the customer that emerge out of our regular routine. Using the concrete finishing case as an example, even though we provided some special service to Frank beyond our regular EMS, we currently have no plan to obtain a fleet of red concrete trucks with electronic sirens and polished aluminum diamond plate, and it may be (we hope) that there will never be another cement finisher that is incapacitated half way through the job. Simply, we don't have any interest in going into the construction business — if, in this case, the workman had been an electrician or a plumber, we would have extended standard medical treatment and then tried to quickly secure the scene (tools, materials, etc.) and then gone back into service. Inherently, copper pipe and aluminum conduit don't have the same loss profile as wet concrete.

The following is a simple, straightforward set of questions each of us should ask and answer to lead us through the empowerment process:

Basic Firefighter Empowerment

Ask yourself:

- Is it the right thing for the customer?
- Is it the right thing for our department?
- Is it legal, ethical, and nice?
- Is it safe?
- Is it on your organizational level?
- Is it something you are willing to be accountable for?
- Is it consistent with our department's values and policies?

....if the answer is yes to all of these questions, don't ask for permission,

JUST DO IT!

This "just do it" empowerment routine is a new trick for a lot of us old fire-officer dogs. This new routine requires us old mutts to begin to take the big scary risk of replacing our traditional control orientation (actually micromanagement) with a new level of enabling and support for those who work under(!) our command. This involves us stepping back from deciding and ordering the details of every action our personnel will take, to encouraging and assisting (actually requiring) the troops to take control of the service delivery process for themselves. This new deal takes advantage of the direct connection the fire company has with the customer and the knowledge they (fire company) have of what is actually required to solve the customer's problem. On the other side, the troops must take responsibility and control for developing the decisions and acquiring and using the resources that are necessary to get the job done. The members of the fire company become the custodians of the service delivery event by effectively representing both the organization and the customers.

In spite of how it sounds, this new way of doing business is not a big, happy, fluffy organizational dance where everyone holds hands and skips along to Camelot. Part of this drill is what empowerment is and what it is not. Effective empowerment connects the customer and the workers in a very practical and problem-solving way. Empowerment requires the organization to clear the obstructions and confusion that can (and do) occur within the relationship between the workers and the organization. Empowerment does not give anyone (anyone!) the ability, access, right, or privilege to treat anyone (anyone!) badly, to break rules or procedures (if they are obsolete, dumb, or dysfunctional, change 'em), or to take negative advantage of any part or person in our system. Simply, empowerment is not a disguise or excuse for not doing your job — in fact, it requires just the opposite!

The empowerment approach is probably the toughest way to package and manage a fire department. It requires everyone to wake up (and join up) and to perform on their level — senior managers operate on the strategic level; middle managers connect and support with a tactical orientation; fire companies directly deliver service and operate on the task level. Many times it's a lot easier to do the job(s) just below you, than what the system is actually paying you to do (like *your* job). Effective empowerment is an enormously mature process that first involves a wake-up call and then a big dose of reality therapy. It's a lot easier on the sending end to give orders to everyone about everything to maintain absolute order and control. It's also a lot easier on the receiving end to work hard, stay low, shuffle your feet, shine your shoes, and shut up. The problem is that this old system simply doesn't cut it any more. The environment is too dynamic. We are called upon to solve a whole new set of problems, and our troops come from the factory wired differently than ever before. There is little room in today's fire service for "ion" firefighters — where the only goals are to get off probat"ion," avoid suspens"ion," and wait for their pens"ion."

The empowerment shift must be started and managed (artfully) by senior managers within the cultural and style context of each individual organization. To be effective, this empowerment shift should occur incrementally over a period of time. It is generally disorienting to the troops when we stodgy old command officers show up with frizzy doos, gold chains, and earth shoes chanting new age stuff and calling everyone under our command "associates." An old dog learning too many new tricks is always suspect so gradual personality change in a positive direction is always much less traumatic on the participants than major overnight personality shifts.

Avoid Unbusinesslike Impressions

Firefighters should attempt to avoid situations that look like the following:

- *Excessively recreational*

    Our service is currently placing a higher emphasis on physical fitness and conditioning programs. Many times our companies

empowerment
Shift-
occurs incrementally
over time.

use public facilities for these activities. These activities are visually obvious to the customers, so we should stick to the fitness script and avoid appearing as if we are just "playing games" or socializing. Aerobic activity is what we are generally doing during these out-of-station forays and such activity should appear to be just that — aerobic. Thirty-five firefighters playing slow motion croquet at the park for two hours is pretty tough to package up in a believable explanation to a taxpayer of how our physical conditioning program is supposed to happen. Conversely, a company jogging thirty minutes at the high school track offers an excellent chance to explain how our fitness program physically prepares our players for show time.

Firefighters are typically high-energy, competitive characters who naturally congregate and do things together. This inclination emerges out of how we do regular team fire fighting. This is basically a very positive approach and feeling, but sometimes when firefighters don't have a fire to fight or an exercise bike to ride and they get together, "horse play" can happen. Company officers must always help underutilized firefighters stay in the businesslike-looking zone.

- *Wrong place — wrong time*

Emergency activity dictates and drives where and when we go and deliver service....simply, we don't have any choice — if the fire is at 5th and Main, we go to 5th and Main. In nonemergency situations, we do have a choice to be strategic, smart, and can control where and when we show up. There are some places/times where a normal customer is going to wonder, not understand, and be confused about our nonemergency presence. Company officers should consider the possible optics of a particular action and then manage that exposure.

It's probably (lots) better to make an appointment for a weekday inspection at 10:00 a.m. and file a "flight plan" with the Battalion Chief to inspect Tassels Topless Go-Go or Chip-n-Dales Bar, than to pull an unannounced visit at midnight on Saturday night.

Mrs. Smith can make sense out of a busy company stopping by a family restaurant, fast food, or take out for lunch (with a portable radio). She probably would wonder and ask about us munching burgers and hanging out with the bad boys at Bubba's Biker Bar and Grill for an hour and a half.

We routinely visit grocery stores to buy hunger prevention supplies. This can create a lot of interest and questions. If we park right next to the front door in the fire lane, block everyone's access, take an hour and a half to stroll through the store to "shop," and then congregate around a cute checkout clerk and giggle at each other for another fifteen minutes, it looks (and is) pretty stupid.

Smart ain't hard when you're hungry....make up a shopping list; delegate getting the goodies; park smart; and leave one member at the rig as a PR agent, question answerer, and lifter of kids into and out of the cab. Get in, shop quickly, be nice, get out, go home — sing while you cook — eat 'til you're sleepy — sleep 'til you're hungry. Making the right choice and managing the impression is generally a pretty simple intelligence test.

- *Hazard Of Excessive Congregation*

  The success of our operations will always depend on having the right players in the right places. Many times this requires that officers identify the number and type of workers who are required to complete a particular operation and then manage the human resources part of the execution process.

  Another part of our response process involves the basic personality of firefighters — smart, aggressive, action oriented, with a high willingness (and capability) to be an active part of the incident action plan. Sometimes, our built-in tactical reserve and our basic profile cause us to overly congregate in a way that appears as an excessive overreaction — or even (more simply), it scares the customer.

  Having 14 firefighters, each with a blaring portable radio in Mrs. Smith's bedroom at 3:00 a.m. on an EMS event is a pretty overwhelming sight, and even a hint that there is work to be done crowds them around her bed more closely. The first officer should evaluate the situation and select the treatment team, assign someone to deal with the family, and assign someone to babysit the pets. The rest of the responders should stage out of the way (probably outside) and be ready to provide any support the IC orders.

  Having a dramatic picture on the front page of the morning paper showing 3 ladder companies, 2 engine companies, and the haz-mat team on the roof of a 950-square-foot house looks like we are having the firefighter's ball in an odd (and not very safe) place....it's pretty tough to make a game look like football if there are 57 players, 12 coaches, 3 bus drivers, and all the cheerleaders milling around on the field at the same time. We need the team that is required to get the job done working directly on that job and the resources required to support the action in standard support positions. We must create and maintain a businesslike balance between too few and too many workers working on the incident.

- *Not Joking In The Wrong Place*

  Firefighters routinely attend and become part of the most difficult, terrifying, and awful events that occur. We deal with trauma, death, and destruction that abruptly disconnects (or even ends) our customer's lives. We are the agency with the resources, skills, and level of operational fitness and experience to deliver urgent physical safety services to those who are typically in the most unfit human condition (confused, hurting, burning, trapped, etc.). Assuming a somewhat detached, professional, clinical approach becomes a major way of surviving a career of attending to human misery and suffering.

Another survival mechanism involves the use of humor as a coping mechanism. Many times this humor ranges from dark to black on the color chart. The point of all this depressing stuff is that we must be careful of where we use what looks and sounds like joking to someone having a real bad day. It may be a careless comment, a joke among the troops, or two adrenaline charged firefighters high fivin' each other in the front yard after knocking down Mrs. Smith's kitchen fire and yelling "good stop" (it probably was) that creates a light-hearted impression to a customer who at that very moment has a very heavy heart.

Most of this behavior is unintentional, but leaves the impression that the event is pretty routine to us — in fact, so routine that we are joking about it or at least around it.

This "be careful" message doesn't mean we can't ever use humor with a customer. It only means we should consider what we say and where we say it and not joke in the wrong place or in the wrong way. Establishing personal contact and using smart, appropriate humor is many times an excellent way to effectively connect and send a positive message to another human. Think before speaking.

- *Keep A Clean Workplace*

As a young firefighter, I always wondered how the city-wide performance evaluation category "appearance of workplace" applied to us. We typically worked in the grungiest, messiest places and at least my workplace appearance (and me) generally looked pretty bad. That old category is starting to make more sense (after 35 years) now that we are looking at customer service in a new, smarter way. Many times our customer can develop a major lasting impression simply on how we leave the place where we delivered service. To some extent, our service delivery signature is the condition of the scene at the end of operations. Simply, this is what we leave the customer in physical terms.

We routinely must manipulate and move buildings, vehicles, equipment, machinery, and landscape to find, extricate, treat, stabilize, package, extinguish, overhaul, shore, dike, dam, and generally interrupt and reverse the incident problem. Lots of times we make lots of mess and if we don't clean up the mess, it can be the gift that keeps giving to our customer.

Leaving a fire scene unsecured and unprotected, with stuff that survived and is okay exposed to and mixed with stuff that is burned and is not okay, is not acceptable. Leaving broken glass all over the sidewalk and driveway, burned furniture thrown out every window leaning up against the side of the structure, and shingles that sailed out in the middle of the street and in the neighbor's yards is also not acceptable. All of these make it appear the fire was controlled by maniacs with water cannons and battering rams, not the professional image we seek to develop.

Littering and leaving a busy intersection after an EMS orgy with 45 pounds of very used medical supplies and a half an acre of bloody rubber gloves looks like we got chased away in the middle of the event.

Rototilling Mrs. Smith's front yard and "aerating" her rose garden with a 1" tip right off the hydrant we checked on her corner will generally cause her to call and indicate how much she appreciates us flushing all that dank, stagnant water out of her personal fire plug.

What happens at the end of a service delivery event currently offers a whole new (and mostly underdeveloped) set of opportunities to send a WOW! message to the customer and to help that person in an important and memorable way. This may include establishing a loss control officer, an owner/occupant support sector, packing belongings in salvage boxes, carefully and gently using small civilized battery-operated construction tools (instead of Godzilla style heavy artillery) to check for fire extension, putting furniture up on small styrofoam blocks so that it doesn't get waterlogged, or a bazillion other positive customer-centered activities that should become a standard part of our approach.

Mom said it all — if you or the event make a mess, clean it up.

Give The Customer Your Undivided Attention

Emergency incidents generally involve some combination of people, places, and things. The combination requires that we rapidly evaluate how the people and things attending our event are connected to and sometimes captured by the event. This situation evaluation involves selecting the critical factors present and quickly going to work on the pieces and parts of the incident problem that will cause it to go away. Our problem elimination approach generally involves doing a set of somewhat separate, but highly-connected activities that take advantage of the earliest incident stage. The smallest (earliest) incident stage will typically produce the largest intervention window of opportunity. For us, fast and effective are inseparable and this means we are always going to do a lot of real quick tactical stuff to establish, retain, and never lose control.

Being preoccupied with initial intervention means we are going to be really busy during the beginning of fire/medical operations, so these front-end stages become a challenging place for us to conduct a customer service program. Obviously, they (the customer) called us to solve an urgent problem and while it's sort of rude to run right past Mrs. Smith on our way to knock down her burning kitchen, it doesn't make much sense to take time at the beginning to explain the magic of combustion while it conducts, radiates, and convects its way down the hallway into her back bedroom. It also doesn't make a whole lot of sense to explain anatomy, physiology, and modern medical electronics to Mrs. Smith before we defib Grandpa Smith. Historically, we have been preoccupied with the tactical part of our job that solved problems directly and physically (more of the hockey team example). This focus was, still is, and probably will always be completely appropriate. Our current customer concern requires we add a new component to our regular incident action planning package. This addition should in no way interfere or interrupt tactical operations — in fact, providing a standard customer support procedure should complement tactical operations. As soon as possible, a team member should be assigned to a regular operational function to establish contact with the customer and to begin to deal with and concentrate on their needs. What is involved in supporting and assisting a customer who is going through a personal emergency becomes fairly standard and can be packaged and managed within our SOP game plan. We are dealing with a person whose life has been interrupted — from being distracted to completely disconnected by some emergency that is profoundly affecting them. They are going through the very personal challenge of not only dealing with what is going on right now, but where do I go and what do I do next? They are generally amateurs at this adjustment process because they are first timers.

On a smaller, very local event, one crew member could play this customer support role in a very simple, straightforward way. This function might be a regular assignment within a team and could be based on rank, personal profile, or rotating assignment. On a larger situation, the IC may establish an owner-occupant support sector who would do larger, longer-term functions to assist and support business owners, larger numbers of displaced and affected customers, or more complicated operational details.

We routinely summon additional resources to perform a variety of functions that are necessary to complete tactical objectives. This resource deployment function is a regular function of the IC. We must add the capability to effectively establish and maintain customer support as a regular part of our standard game plan and add this to the list of reasons we call for more help where required. The objective of this approach is really pretty simple — the organization must consider the personal situation and needs of our customers in the planning process just like every other tactical and task oriented function and then play that way at show time.

About ten years ago our service woke up to the reality that our own department members required professional critical incident recovery assistance to help keep the bats out of our belfry. This (long overdue) wake-up call related to a group of experienced professionals (us) who got up in the morning and sort of expected they might have to do some pretty tough stuff that day. Imagine what is going on with Mrs. Smith as she watches essentially everything that defined her entire existence going up in the thermal column. Setting her (by herself) on the curb across the street to watch this spectacle clearly looks and is low rent (big understatement) and does not come anywhere close to matching today's stage of fire service development.

When you're confused, beat up, and hurting, nothing feels as good as some calm, capable, credible, concerned person paying attention to you, and there is no attention like undivided, exclusive attention.

Don't Act Like Delivering Service Is An Inconvenience To You

This modest essay has so far exhausted the faithful reader, making and remaking the point that customer service delivery is the most human (firefighter) directed and dependent activity we engage in. How requests for emergency service occur and how our members react to that occurrence within our schedule and routine becomes a major factor in how that customer contact turns out.

We essentially have a very retail relationship with our customers. We receive and respond to requests for service one at a time. It's impossible for us to store our service in a centrally located warehouse and then deliver that service along a prearranged route and schedule. While we know some overall activity trends, each separate request for emergency service is driven by the emergency episode itself, and we have no real capability to predict or schedule when or where the customer will need us. How our nonemergency activity is scheduled and how we feel about that schedule necessarily conditions how we deliver service.

Our nonemergency support activity is scheduled and conducted typically within regular department program packages. These programs are scheduled and conducted mostly during the day. At meal times we cook, eat, clean up, and ponder digestion. During the evening we do upright (sitting) standby (chairs pointed directly toward TV). At night we do prone position standby. Fire companies predictably develop habits around their company routine and a mentality that revolves around how that work is scheduled and performed.

The overall objective of virtually every fire department support program activity is to create and maintain an effective state of readiness to deliver some service to a customer. This reality applies to both fire companies (who extend actual service delivery along with some support activities) and support personnel (whose regular job is to do support stuff). A big-time problem can occur when we lose sight of that reality. The objective of the support program is not the program itself, but how that activity assists what we have to do at show time to protect the customer. This program confusion involves the very simple fact that we are always doing something — scheduled/unscheduled, active/sedentary, conscious/unconscious. It's impossible for us to put ourselves into a "do nothing" state (although we had two B-shifters who came close), so every call for service interrupts something else we are doing and requires we stop that activity to respond to the customer. If we lose the focus that our real (and only) business is to respond to customer's requests for service, we can develop a negative reaction when a call for service interrupts what we are doing.

Fire department managers must make customer service the highest priority and most important activity the organization engages in. Customer service standards should be developed, measured, and positively reinforced. Good performance should be recognized, commended and, celebrated; performance problems should be coached for correction. Managers should send a clear message to department members that the organization will not accept substandard customer outcomes. Customer service must be the ultimate test of why we are doing any other departmental activity — if what we are doing does not relate directly or indirectly to the delivery of service, we should question why we are doing it.

It becomes pretty difficult to cover up the feeling that the call for service is either a distraction or an inconvenience to us when we deal with the author of the call — the customer. That inconvenienced reaction can involve subtle but clear messages like sarcasm, critical looks, impatient expressions, and negative body language. Or more explicit, and really dumb, reactions like, "You called us for this during Monday night football?" (true story).

A lot of our daily activity is very enjoyable and we are lucky to have a job that allows us to watch TV, eat meals with our buddies, work out, play games, go nighty night, etc. We are able to do these things because they do not interfere with our response availability....simply, they are interruptible.

When we become so attached to those nonemergency programs that we feel they are the reason we are in business and then act out those feelings, we need a serious jolt of reality therapy. Mrs. Smith could care less that what is an emergency to her interrupted a critical installment of our favorite soap opera series.

A Customer Service — ultimate test of why we are doing any other departmental activity.

Don't disqualify the
customer with your
qualifications.

6.
Don't disqualify the customer with your qualifications.

Service Delivery Changes

Everything we have discussed so far has formed a description of a service delivery system that is designed, managed, and operated to maintain the highest possible level of response readiness. We realize that the protection needs of the customer and the community range on a scale from very minor to very severe. This reality creates a typical fire department system design and operational mentality based on worst case scenario planning — firefighters are just naturally pessimistic — we continually (and obsessively) plan, prepare, and practice for the "big one." We are located, equipped, trained, organized, and staffed to respond to and perform under the most difficult, dangerous, and demanding circumstances.

Our operational versatility emerges (or sort of works backward) from the capability to deal with the most severe situation — if we can assemble the big guns required to fight a war, it's pretty easy for that same system to reload smaller caliber ammunition to handle a little street fight. To be effective, firefighters must be able to operate anywhere on the severity scale and must customize an incident action plan to match and overpower the incident profile.

This traditional "think big" mentality and the resources that come with that approach formed the backdrop and basis for a set of productivity driven changes that have occurred, particularly within the urban fire service, over the past two decades. These changes have challenged our ability to balance our concentration between the smaller end of the service delivery scale and maintaining the simultaneous capability of delivering larger, more complex operations....the present is a lot more complicated (and bewildering) than the past — stand by for the future.

The local government productivity improvement emphasis (craze) that occurred in the early 1970s (big time in Phoenix) directed us to consider other uses and services for our in-place existing resources. This productivity movement has produced a twenty-year period of active change, increased service delivery versatility, and dynamic improvement in the response, versatility, capability, and effectiveness of our business.

In addition to improving the delivery of traditional fire control services (ICS, firefighter safety, positive pressure ventilation, Class A foam,

etc.), we are currently very actively involved in ALS-BLS level emergency medical and transport services, haz-mat mitigation, special technical rescue operations, and a variety of other educational, prevention, and community involvement programs. While these service delivery improvements have involved major changes in our tools, equipment, and procedures, the most dramatic change in our business has related to the organizational investment we have made in increasing the skill level and sophistication of our firefighters.

Firefighter Profile

The basic ingredient in any substantive fire service change necessarily involves the behavior and performance capability of our human resources. Our service delivery process is effective to the extent our firefighters are effective (that sort of says it all). The productivity changes that started in the '70s created a new combination of both how we did our jobs and a need to change how we felt about doing those new functions. Our service had a lot of experience in changing behaviors, but changing feelings and emotions is a whole new deal — providing service to real live customers is a lot different than protecting buildings (buildings don't have feelings)....simply being grumpy with a customer generally gets a different reaction, effect (and phone call), than being grumpy with an immovable inanimate object (like a building). We have been (and will continue to be) successful in meeting the change challenge because we started with extraordinary human resources.

Firefighters today are an interesting combination of the new and the old. Recent improvements in entry qualifications, lots better training, standard fire fighting, medical, and special rescue qualifications and certifications, continuing education, and program management progress have greatly increased the personal capability of firefighters to deliver new, different, and better service.

A lot of old stuff is also still going on. Firefighters are still highly inclined to directly engage the problem, articulate their feelings with action, and attempt to meet whatever challenge is present. They love commitment and hate compromise. They regard tactical problems as the competitive opponent of their professional capability and are highly inclined to aggressively outexecute or outplay any challenge. They are willing to approach and get close to hazards that are causing problems. The command system must generally pull them out, not push them in. Firefighters are typically loaded for bear, have an attitude, and will willingly pick a fight with a problem. They are attracted to strong, straightforward leadership and are not much inclined to follow a committee into battle.

Our members voluntarily enter the service and commit themselves to a career with a cultural/spiritual tradition that directs us to take enormous risks, if necessary, to protect a person we have never met and do not know. The willingness of firefighters to put their own welfare on the line for an unknown, threatened customer is a unique characteristic in a service delivery relationship.

They come on duty prepared and programmed to do whatever it takes to get the job done, including jumping into the conditions that exist on the worst end of the scale. This admirable set of firefighter characteristics and qualities gets mixed up with some other current events that produce an interesting paradox.

System Access

An important element in this paradox relates to the quick and easy access the customers still have to our services. We ask only two basic questions that quickly trigger our response:

#1. "Where are you?" and,

#2. "What's the matter?"

No forms, applications, paperwork, or interviews with mindless bureaucrats. Simply, answer #1 and #2 — we're out the door (hopefully it's all the way up). The newest enhanced addition to most 911 systems (E911) even eliminates the need to answer question #1. The basic, original system was built during the old days, when we delivered mostly fire control services. When a customer smelled smoke and called us, there was (and still is) a pretty simple and straightforward physical problem going on....even today, fire control jobs have more clarity and less confusion than any other service delivery category.

Our customers have predictably become aware of the wider variety of other (than just fire) services we now deliver. They have utilized these services very actively. For example, for much of the American fire service the majority (70% to 80%) of our current response activity now relates to emergency medical services. This activity shift has caused the call receipt and dispatch process that occurs at the front end of the event to become a lot more involved and complicated. Attempting to sort out the details of a request for service relating to a medical, welfare, or other human support service problem requires a lot different caller information gathering and dispatch approach than the very straightforward way we used to answer the old alarm room phone, "Where's the fire?"

In spite of the current service delivery changes and complications, two basic initial deployment pieces have remained about the same. First, initial access to our system is still easy and quick. In most places and cases, dial three digits 9-1-1, and we answer on the first ring. Secondly, we still don't have much effective capability (or interest) to screen out requests for service. Given our basic concern for the customer's welfare along with today's screwy legal/liability environment and our basic pessimistic approach, if the caller says they need help, we send it.

Teaching Old Trucks New Tricks

Another piece of the paradox involves the use of old resources to deliver new services. As we evolved into the delivery of more human-

centered services (as opposed to just protecting buildings), we forgot to review and revise our hardware inventory. The big productivity improvement involved taking advantage of a workforce, which is the most expensive part of our system (85% of the bucks), that in the 1970s had space in their schedule to deliver more/different/better services. This workforce came with a very traditional fleet of fire fighting apparatus that was and still is in place. We sent the firefighters to school to change their skill level and to prepare them for how they would look in the future. We forgot to send the fire trucks (figuratively) to school so that they could also develop an idea of how they should look in that same future.

The effect of this imbalance is that the firefighters (humans) changed a lot — the trucks (hardware) stayed essentially the same. We are now delivering mostly EMS on the most recent up-to-date models of traditional engine and ladder apparatus. These units are absolutely essential for fire control activity that continues to be an important and essential service (in fact, fire is still our middle name).

The paradox part of the new system occurs when we struggle to fit a nonfire EMS or customer service request into the engine/ladder profile, particularly when the event is not serious. When we mount up on the fire-tank, we typically leave the station expecting to fight bears (major league event) and end up finding a medical emergency that features a bunny with a run-down battery (minor league event). This situation sets up a reaction where we begin to define that call (service delivery request) as a small-time unenergized rabbit (customer) abusing a system that is designed to fight big-time bears. This is where we struggle to get old equipment (along with our old mentality) to do what is essentially a new job that the traditional piece of rolling stock (and our original mentality) was not originally designed to do. Simply, a 1500 GPM centrifugal pump or a 100-foot hydraulically operated aerial ladder really doesn't directly connect with a customer who has sprained an ankle. While the old time equipment is a part of the system, it was designed for fire control, not delivering medical, social, and support services. While this may be a big deal to us as insiders, it really doesn't affect the customer much. In most cases, the customer actually having the problem could care less if we get to them on a spaceship, a ladder truck, or a pogo stick — when they need us they want us to get there quickly, solve the problem, and be nice. The point of the old equipment/new service paradox is that we now have enough smarts and experience with alternative EMS vehicles to know that they make a lot of sense for our service. As an example, parking a ladder tender (small squad body, four-door cab) that carries

EMS and fire fighting tools next to a big boy 100-foot senior tillered aerial and empowering the company officer to hop on the right one based on the type of call for service makes lots of sense (Phoenix has eleven of them....huge success).

Customer Profile

Today, many of our customers relate to and use our response system in a very different way than before. They have developed an awareness and understanding that we have a wider service delivery capability, and they have become more familiar and skillful at calling for those services. Today, they see us (and use us) in a much more full-service way than the old fire-only perspective. A major aspect of this change has been to not only dramatically increase our overall activity but also to greatly expand our customer base.

In the past, we generally encountered and dealt with customers that came with burning buildings. We have always had a very special concern and reaction to fire customers. We strongly feel that our response is absolutely essential and appropriate whenever there is any existence or even suspicion that a fire is present. In fact, in most urban places, there is enabling legislation (local ordinance — generally in the fire code) that requires the fire department be summoned by the owner/occupant if a fire is discovered. Today, the vast majority of our services are delivered directly to humans, not to a building or mechanical process. These "new" customers have caused a major change (that is still going on) that requires we effectively develop the skill and understanding to relate to a wide variety of people throughout the community. Some of these customers use our services in very non-traditional ways based on their socioeconomic status, ability to solve problems themselves, access to resources, basic intelligence, and overall sanity and stability — this covers pretty much all of us at various times in our lives. We have become in many ways the response agency of first resort and the response agency of last resort. Simply, at 3:30 a.m., when Mrs. Smith's hot water heater decides to blast its bottom off, and she is home alone and the water level is at her ankles and rising — who else does she call? When that occurs, we have the very real option of regarding the event as an opportunity or an inconvenience.

The Crux of the Paradox

The quick, easy, and nonbureaucratic access that customers currently have to our system sets up a process where they (the customer) get to define their own emergency. Although their problem may be critical to them, many times it is actually only a marginally urgent condition. Our response and deployment system becomes vulnerable to the difference between what the customer tells the dispatcher (based on the customer's "amateur" perceptions) and what the firefighters actually encounter on the scene (based on their "professional" capability and experience).

Another characteristic of our response system is that we have only one on-duty/available workforce and that workforce is dispersed in fire stations throughout the community. We have full-service firefighters organized in teams who respond to whatever occurs in their first-due (franchise) area. We don't have one group who only responds to big fires and another group who only goes to minor fires; we don't have a group of medics who only go on heavy-duty trauma and another group who specialize in cut fingers....and, we don't have a special hot water heater cleanup crew.

Delivering service in an environment where our members must operate every place and any place on the incident scale with regard to the type and severity of what they must deal with requires a new level of versatility, maturity, patience, understanding, and good nature.

This entire service delivery shift has created an occupational paradox that presents a current challenge. It goes something like this:

- We have greatly increased the skill level and service delivery capability of our firefighters and our entire response system.

- This increase has given us the foundation to advertise and expand our ability to deliver new services — particularly medical, welfare, and support programs.

- Our members come on duty prepared to use a full range of their technical skills and abilities. Only serious problems require they use their most advanced capabilities.

- Our customers are now using these services more and more.

- Sometimes our customers call us for problems that our members do not define as serious or critical.

- In the vast majority of cases, whatever the customer called us for is an emergency to them — regardless of how we redefine their situation.

- If our customers are really beat up as a result of a serious problem, our firefighters regard that situation as a "righteous" call; if the problem is minor, there is a temptation to define the event as a "snivel" call — a big-time problem occurs when our members act out that "snivel" definition.

- All of this mushes together in a way that our firefighters, who are typically more qualified (actually, a lot more) than ever before, develop a judgment that some of our customers are less qualified than ever before, because their problem did not come up to the firefighter's training/skill level or the expectations or qualifications they have for an authentic, legitimate customer (or event).

- When this occurs, our firefighters disqualify those people as customers and can begin to treat them in a callous, indifferent, sometimes rude, and disrespectful manner.

- If this process occurs frequently enough over a period of time, our reputation goes from being heroes to being jerks....as we lose customer support, acceptance, and affection, our organization begins to decline.

Here on paper, it is pretty easy to take a deep breath and lay out a nice neat paradox and then apply a little sophomoric deductive logic that is very clinical, clear, detached, and simple. The problem with this simple approach is that it may really be too simplistic. The challenge we currently face in delivering very personal service to the entire (sometimes undressed and ugly) body politic may be the most difficult service delivery change (and challenge) we have taken on since Ben set us up.

It's a lot more straightforward and familiar for us to rescue and remove a customer who is in the very dark part of the shadow of death

 because they are in a fire-involved compartment than it is to respond to the needs of some customers. An 80-year-old customer tells the dispatcher at 3:30 a.m. that she has a crushing chest pain radiating down her left arm. When the closest BLS unit, ALS backup, and an ambulance (10 firefighters in attendance) arrive, they discover her problem is she can't turn off her clock radio (true story). Each firefighter has been on duty 19½ hours, hasn't been to bed, and has already gone on 14 calls. There is an enormous (and understandable) temptation to turn off her radio with a pick-head axe, reprimand her for terminal stupidity, and slam the door behind us. As the firefighters who were actually on this call told the insane old Fire Chief (in a customer service meeting), "Don't worry Chief, we turned off her radio, did her hair, and two loads of wash(!)." This is WOW! service delivery in the most difficult situation and setting. To acknowledge their heroic action, we should (always) hang a gold medal around the necks of both the fire fighting team who saved the shadow-of-death fire customer and the medic team who was really nice when they helped a lonely, somewhat deranged, not too functional old lady at 3:30 in the morning.

I have been attempting to somehow figure out, understand, and write about fire service reality for almost 40 years. The lessons never end, regardless of longevity and persistence. I have never used the word "paradox" before (other than to describe two M.D.'s). When I ponder the use of that somewhat unusual (to us) word in the context of our current situation and challenge, I come up with the following reflection about having a long-term customer relationship. I (a typical customer) have gone into a hardware store and bought two ³⁄₁₆" x 2¼" machine screws from a friendly, helpful, nuts-and-bolts guy. Later, I went back and bought an $1,150 table saw. I took my car (that I thought was out of order) into a Chevy dealer to get it repaired. It wasn't broken. They thanked me for coming in, didn't charge me, and wished me well. Later, I went back and bought a $28,000 Suburban. I went into a restaurant and ordered a glass of iced tea. The entire restaurant crew treated me like I had ordered a 10-course meal. Later, I went back and took 55 people to dinner.

I guess the point of all this is that we, as both individuals and as an organization, probably send a stronger message and define ourselves to the customer more when they don't need us badly, as when they do. In fact, many times the customers who need firefighters really, really badly, either don't know what is going on or they don't survive what is going on that gets us involved. It's pretty tough to run a service business when all your "authentic" customers are unconscious or die. Sooner or later, the customer will need us. Sooner or later, we will need the customer. If we disqualify the customer in the short term, they will disqualify us in the long term....we should all reread and reflect on the last sentence, if we want to stay in business.

Basic organizational
behavior must become
customer-centered.

7.
Basic organizational behavior must become customer-centered.

We have discussed the various parts of the service delivery system required to consistently produce standard problem-solving customer service. Each separate element involves a somewhat different set of people, activities, and approach. *Quick* requires us to concentrate on our basic deployment and how we maintain consistent, fast, backed-up system status and response. *Effective* involves managing and refining the action parts of the system. *Skillful* is the product of paying attention to the programming and practice of our firefighters. *Safe* involves strong procedures, smart discipline, and application. *Caring* is the result of positive, progressive, sensible, humane, everyday management that emerges out of a thoughtful, decent organizational philosophy. *Managed* comes from applying sound, modern principles that get the best from the organization and its human resources.

To be consistently effective, these somewhat separate activities must line up in a flexible, but connected formation, all directed (pointed) toward delivering service to a customer. This organizational approach makes the customer the focal point of all organizational activity and centralizes our individual and collective effort. The answer to almost every organizational question must in some way include the customer. In fact, if the customer doesn't show up in the answer, we should ask ourselves why we are screwing around with whatever the question was about (if you attend a meeting where "customer" is not mentioned in the first 15 minutes — leave).

[handwritten margin note: Customer = 15 min — leave]

Creating and maintaining a central customer focus becomes a difficult, ongoing leadership challenge. There are many distractions, barriers, and interruptions that naturally occur in just getting everyone who is directly and indirectly involved in the delivery of service through the day. Many organizational support activities have a beginning, a middle, and an end all to themselves. A lot of those activities don't directly connect with a customer, and it's pretty easy for those who are responsible for those functions to lose track of how what they do ultimately connects with Mrs. Smith.

Given the typical compression from every direction that typically occurs in management jobs, it is particularly easy on that level for us poor souls (chiefs) to have the trees begin to obscure the forest. Currently there is an incredible amount of management development stuff available. Any fire officer with a mailbox generally gets $3\frac{1}{2}$ pounds of

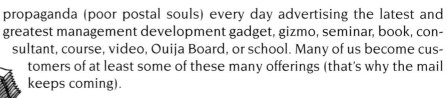

propaganda (poor postal souls) every day advertising the latest and greatest management development gadget, gizmo, seminar, book, consultant, course, video, Ouija Board, or school. Many of us become customers of at least some of these many offerings (that's why the mail keeps coming).

If a hundred years of intense management and organizational development, an almost endless array of inspirational platform speakers, a bazillion pulp trees that paid the supreme sacrifice to become management self-help/how-to books, all the MBA-MPA graduate education in creation, or the virtual army of management consultants (who at this very moment are winging their way to their next client) do not in some way assist, facilitate, support, or help workers and their bosses to more effectively deliver service directly to a real live customer, then their effort and effect is plain, garden-variety moonshine.

The preceding very aerobic paragraph is not meant to trivialize or demean how important sound management technology and technique is to effective organizational operation. Clearly, we must continually use current management development to keep up. We must never stop going to school (not necessarily in a classroom) and listening to those who can inspire us. We must read, read, read, and read some more. Sometimes bringing in a smart outsider with "new eyes" can clear away enough trees for us to get a glimpse of the forest. Whether all this activity becomes management gold that is directive or it becomes management mumbo-jumbo that is just distracting, is up to local organization leaders.

These leaders must attend, pay attention, reflect, and refine what is currently out in the management development environment to somehow sort out the beef from the baloney. They must then package up and apply the good stuff to where Engine One and Mrs. Smith come together. The point of the entire management development drill is to improve actual service delivery — not to drink seminar coffee in the lobby of a two-star hotel and mentally masturbate in a highly collaborative manner with industry peers (current word = networking).

The entire organization must become directed by the simple, timeless, and primitive reality that Mrs. Smith is why we are in business. Anyone in the food chain who loses that customer-centered focus is taking their organizational room and board under false pretenses (sorry about that).

Lots of Empire-State-Building-sized egos, useless/pointless power games, executive insecurity, micromanagement control freaks with 25 years of severe toilet training, and goofy leaders who lost their way along the way currently exist in many fire departments. They create a detached and deranged internal environment where workers and bosses on the line deliver service in spite of and not because of these lost souls. Sadly, many are stumbling around toward the top of the fire service chain of command.

We must recognize that basic fire department customer service delivery on the business end involves three major players: workers, bosses, and customers. The customers are those who receive service or are in some way connected to the event. Workers are firefighters who operate on the task level. They do the skilled manual labor that directly solves the customer's problem. Bosses are first level supervisor company officers who personally and directly manage and lead the service delivery event. These three players are intensely connected operationally and come together right where service is delivered. While there are a lot of other people and places required to create the READY, GET SET, only workers and their bosses can do the GO part of the organizational service delivery operation.

An absolutely essential fire department customer service player is the company officer boss. They are typically Captain and Lieutenant types who do first level supervision as an integral (inside) part of the service delivery team — right where and when the service delivery event occurs. They don't need to make a phone call to get permission, check a form or a computer screen, deal with a middleman (or woman), or look up in the ops manual to determine what is going on. They can directly see, touch, feel, hear, smell, and sense the activity, progress, and outcome of service delivery as it is actually occurring.

Company officers operate inside the basic fire department service delivery team — the fire company. They are the only bosses with continuous access and control of the fire company peer process (the most powerful organizational influence). Their presence and effect are so consistently powerful because they are with the vast majority of a fire department's human resources all the time.

They sit next to you at dinner. They ride in the shotgun spot, talk on the radio, and blast the air horn. They are the last person you see when you get up to go to the head and first person you see when you get back. He/she is as cold/hot, clean/dirty, sad/happy, hungry/full, wet/dry, up/down as their company members....simply, you can run, but you can't hide (as Joe Louis said). We break into the fire service at the booter (rookie) end of the fire company where we make the coffee, raise the flag, and ride backwards. Our first, and in most cases, most important boss is a company officer because he/she gets to touch the clay (us) while it's soft. We pay our dues by working our way through our basic work group — the fire company. Our development and experience as a company member prepares us to become a company boss. When we make that change (promotion), typically we move over in the front seat 3½ feet to the right. Company officers don't "emerge" from MBA programs....they emerge directly out of fire companies. You can fool the spectators, but you can't fool the players. You can jive the BC when he/she stops by to deliver the mail and get a sick leave form signed. The Fire Chief down at the Puzzle Palace occasionally sees your name on a roll call and gets a warm glow. The Mayor and City Manager still think Engine One is the first car of a freight train. The Shadow and your Captain know what actually lurks in the hearts of firefighters.

The Captain on Engine One also is the only person in the organizational food chain who can directly control the service delivery event at Mrs. Smith's at 3:00 a.m. The officer can directly support and reinforce effective action and directly coach and redirect action that is out of balance. Everything that occurs ahead of the event is important preparation. Everything after can be useful review. No one else in the system has the 3:00 a.m. control except the company officer. The 3:00 a.m. roll call looks something like this: the Fire Chief (who just completed a 40-hour total quality management seminar) is tucked in with his bear and blanky; the quality control guy/gal (who has a stunningly effective measurement matrix) is nighty-night with visions of Baldridge Awards dancing in his/her head; the Mayor (who now routinely calls voters customers) is unconscious, having nocturnal fantasies about being Governor; and the Battalion Chief (who routinely practices space-age management) is stuck on the opposite side of Mrs. Smith's, looking at the wrong side of a 250-car freight train that is slowing on its way to Bolivia. Very simply, we live or die (sometimes literally) on the brains, guts, and on-line direction of the company officer.

All the TQM, organizational development, and strategic planning saints and angels preaching and pontificating until the 4th of July, and then waving the flag for customer service, can't have a fraction of the effect of an on-line company officer who walks the walk of the effective customer service game plan right where and when it occurs.

As a young firefighter, the author (very lucky) worked for such a company officer. He was smart, tough, and nice. He was the Chairman of the Board of the business of our company and he minded that business. He had a crew cut and on one arm (very big) he had "U.S.M.C." and on the other "Mom." (Those tats provided a quick and accurate snapshot of him.) He hadn't gone to graduate school, so he talked in nice, short, understandable sentences. If he liked what you were doing, he told you to keep doing it. If he wanted you to start doing something, he told you to start. If he wanted you to stop doing something, he told you to stop. He listened to his crew, took care of us, and brought out the best in everyone. He was very patient with mistakes as long as they were new ones. Virtually everyone who worked for him got promoted (or else).

He had the simple, straightforward expectation that his company would do whatever work was required for as long as it took to get the job done. You didn't stop fighting until the fire was all the way out (and then some).

Probably the most powerful thing about him was he always modeled his own expectations. He had the brains, experience, and stature to manage mightily without micromanaging. He established high quality standards for his company and then patrolled the perimeter of those standards without ever raising his voice. I started working for him in 1959, and he had what looked like (to a baby firefighter) old-fashioned values, but he was (and still is) as modern (actually timeless) as anyone I have ever known. He was one of those rare people who went through the human assembly line when everything was going really well. It must have been Wednesday morning when the workers were happy and oriented. They used all the right parts and all the parts fit together. They made him out of all real stuff with no artificial junk. He was, like a lot of really exceptional people, not so much an ordinary person with something added as he was a regular person with nothing taken away. He simply was a complete, intact person and the boss from heaven.

NOTE:

I use the term "boss" (throughout this booklet) with the realization that it is a somewhat outdated and perhaps even politically incorrect term in the most contemporary context. The reason I use it is that to me, no other word describes the special online relationship and connection that exists between the boss, the workers, and the work (customer). I was raised to believe that everyone both needs a boss and has a boss. Through the years, I have seen a lot of problems occur when folks forget that reality — a lot of really effective stuff happens when we remember it. I have also noticed that bosses are so influential (actually powerful — another politically incorrect word) that the difference between a good boss and a bad boss is closely connected to occupational heaven and hell. The reader can certainly substitute any other word that works for them.

What he did so consistently and naturally was to be an extraordinary example of what being customer-centered actually (not theoretically or academically) means. He didn't talk about it much — he just did it. If his crew was nice to a customer, he just smiled (we liked it a lot when he did that). If the situation (or us) got intense, he stopped smiling and put his hand on your shoulder and helped you. If he sensed you were getting impatient, feeling grumpy or rude, or in any way unprofessional, he put his hand on your shoulder and squeezed (we didn't like it when he did that). If the customer got ugly with us, he patiently smiled and reasoned with them. If he sensed the customer was going to get physical with us, he put his hand on their shoulder and squeezed (they didn't like it when he did that). The ongoing application of his standard for taking care of the customer (and us) in the street became a way of company life.

Our company was a downtown engine company and a lot of our customers were on the down side of the luck scale. The problems that went along with their environment were typically not very elegant (to say the least). Simply, there was a lot of wear and tear and not much maintenance on those who lived in that environment. He would interact with someone at a buck-a-night flop house as if we had responded to the Ritz. Many times I would have cheerfully strangled (stopped by fear of shoulder trauma) some deranged knight of the road whose problem at 3:00 a.m. was that Martians were entering his body through his navel and the spaceship was spinning brodies (360's) on his pancreas (or wherever).

He would listen patiently, send one of us to find a piece of cardboard for a navel shield, put it over the guy's belly, and explain that he had plugged up the intergalactic super highway. He would tuck Mr. Spaceship in and we would go back to the station.

He would explain to us (but more importantly he would show us) that life was tough at the Ajax Rooms, and who knows, maybe Martians were really going to make their power play from the guy's belly button. He showed us that some folks don't have much going for them to begin with and emergencies are pretty democratic and unforgiving and tend to equalize anyone and everyone. He showed us that our performance and behavior could make a big difference in our customer's lives. While he would never (ever) preach to us, him saying in his own very basic street-oriented way that up and in is really pretty close to down and out, stayed with a dumb kid who was trying to figure out what end of the line the water comes out and the meaning of life all at the same time. Strong company officer bosses like him have the ongoing opportunity to move customer-centered from a theory we talk about to an actual outcome we can practice and see.

Currently, it's pretty popular and looks modern to beat the customer-centered drum. The problem is, it's a lot harder for us to consistently pull it off than to just blab about it. Most of us fire service managers are the product of a 200-year tradition that has regarded those who needed and received our services as "fire victims." We have basically concentrated on the system, approach, and mentality required to conduct the heavy-duty hydraulic and tactical support operations required to physically control fires in structures. While we have always been concerned about and nice to "fire victims," we basically regarded them as accessories that came with burning buildings. During prefire planning excursions, we would look into the windows of the buildings in our first-due area, right past the people in those buildings, and try to fantasize how the building (and us) would react under fire conditions. During actual operations, we would interrupt the fire fighting routine long enough to rescue and quickly stabilize anyone who the fire beat up, and then get on with our regular fire fighting routine. We have all at one time or another had victim status bestowed upon us as the result of a lot of different dismal reasons. It's generally not nearly as much fun as a day at the park. Victims typically lose control over any options or choices that relate to their welfare or best interests. Our role is to serve as their advocate during what is generally a negative ordeal that has put them in a very vulnerable position/condition. Then we must, as quickly and effectively as possible, return control back to them so that they can make the personal decisions that return control to them so that they can get back to normal.

Fire fighting is an action-oriented, contact sport that feels good to the participants. Fire fighting is the activity that provides the most primitive way that we complete the circuit of our identity. Our most defining and overriding reality is where fire and water come together. In many cases and places, we have a lot longer term connection before, during, and after the fire with the structure than we do with the humans involved with the event.

most defining reality
fire and water
come together

In fact, we attempt (very appropriately) as quickly as possible to move any nonfire people out of the hot/warm zone. As we do this, we are typically bundled up in ugly, yellow, fire-resistive murf suits, wheezing through SCBA facepieces — not exactly a real friendly costume to wear when you're trying to establish a close, warm, personal relationship with a customer.

We have historically approached our jobs in a highly manipulative (using tools and equipment), technical, and mechanical way and we probably always will. We are the local agency who responds and operates to interrupt and control fires and other emergencies. Our strength is, and always has been, our capability to quickly deliver teams of highly motivated workers who together do organized, coordinated, skillful manual labor within a rapidly shrinking and dynamic window of opportunity. Being customer-centered means that we continue doing the physical stuff, while we add (both actually and symbolically) a new customer service manual in our system. This manual is inserted ahead of and integrated with our old drill manual, which describes our basic work evolutions (hose, ladder, tools), and our SOP manual that outlines our operational formations and moves (command and control). The new customer-centered approach becomes a highly complementary (not competitive) partner of our traditional service delivery system. The combination forms a very effective balance between taking care of both the human and physical needs of the incident. Customer-centered fire service organizational behavior emerges out of the following changes:

- The customer must appear (for the first time) in both our organizational design and mentality right next to fire company workers and their bosses. The organization must now surround and no longer geometrically and philosophically separate the fire companies (and customer) from the policy and support part of the organization. This design change must become a planned, practical approach that involves a long-term organizational shift in re-direction, commitments, and investments.

- Customer-centered means that customer needs, perceptions, and feelings begin to design and drive how the service delivery system looks and behaves. This change requires we include a new dimension of customer consideration as a natural value added piece of our regular problem-solving routine. The current, big-deal word for such changes — paradigm shift — will require and involve a scary change from the traditional vanilla, chocolate, and strawberry, to a new 31 flavors of fire service delivery. We have always done the very best we could for our customers, but we haven't spent much time asking them what they really want....simply, we decided what we thought they really needed, delivered that service, and went home.

- In the brave new customer-centered world we are constructing, it will be necessary for firefighters to come from the factory with a basic characteristic of liking people and an overriding inclination and desire to help those people. We must develop a system to attract, recruit, test, train, place, and support such candidates who can survive a career of intense service delivery to folks having a really bad day. Firefighters without this basic inclination and skill should take up smoke jumping into wilderness areas where they can commune with bears and spotted owls — simply, fire service work in the city will be far too human intensive for these grizzly souls.

- Delivering service today is becoming more complex and requires that we combine some new stuff with the old. While solving the main problem will always be the basis of our service delivery system, we must now begin to widen our view and move away from the inclination (tunnel vision) to focus exclusively on the major incident problem. While the main problem is what gets us and the customer together, that problem typically creates another whole set of other personal and family challenges for our customer(s). If we are prepared and inclined to deal only with the technical/tactical part of the event, we necessarily will leave those other parts unsolved when we disappear from the scene. Another way we can short change the customer (and ourselves) occurs when we evaluate our effectiveness only on the outcome of the main core service we delivered. In some cases we attend and operate on human and physical situations with a defensive outcome for those (and what) is directly involved....simply, sometimes the customer dies or the building burns down. Most of these situations leave a lot of people and confusion behind. These survivors are also our customers. We must begin to assume responsibility to deliver service to the entire situation. Our involvement in virtually every situation should extend beyond solving only the major incident problem.

This approach is not meant to be all things to all people. It basically means that we must assist our customers, whose lives have been in some way disconnected by a problem that has brought us together, with the next step(s) to reconstruct their lives. No other agency is able to do this in the way that we can. The customer has come through our regular system (911), we are present, we know the most about the customer's problem, and we have developed a relationship with that customer.

Most every firefighter has packed up and returned to quarters to wait for the next alarm and left a vacationing family with a burned out van standing along the side of a busy expressway, a burned out family sitting across the street from their recently vaporized home, or a catatonic, grief-stricken family standing around a bed with a sheet pulled over a loved one. Today, there is no way to package up these traditional responses so that they make sense (or in a way that we can be very proud of them). We know better and we can do better. We must develop the habitual inclination and capability to evaluate and approach our customer's events in a holistic way that considers a full range of the needs that come with that situation. We must also provide our troops with the systems, training, and support required to actually provide those services in the street. A lot of those services will require that we effectively connect our customers with other agencies who can provide medium-range social and support services. This will require fire service leaders to develop and service different and better relationships with these other agencies. All of these changes move being customer-centered from blab to action.

- Historically, the American fire service has used a vertical, power-based military model where authority was the main organizational influence. The model is pretty simple — authority is a function of rank. Those who have rank have authority. Their basic role is to control those who have neither (rank or authority). The boss is in the center of this old model, and the organization is in place (in effect) to basically deliver service to itself (the boss). Leaders must now vacate the center of the system to let the customer in. Simply, the highest profile (and status) part of the system must become the connection between the workers (fire company) and the customers. Leaders must replace artificial rank-induced control with genuine service delivery support. In this new system, we must stop playing in our own organizational poop and work for the customers. Today's management environment requires that leaders play nicely and share the toys in a completely new way. Rather than acquiring, guarding, and expanding the traditional organizational goodies that make us fearless leaders so breathless (power, influence, authority, respect, love, etc.), today's leaders give those same capabilities away to the troops. This sharing creates a "boomerang" effect where empowered workers not only become more and more effective, but also give those same capabilities back to the bosses — plus some extra. The "boomerang" process is really pretty simple. Bosses empower workers on the task level. Workers extend respect, support, and cooperation (empowerment) back up the line to bosses on the strategic level. This new process lets everyone win and makes the old-time (military) officer's instruction manual very obsolete. How our service continues to expand the effectiveness and capability of our human resources will depend directly on how today's leaders catch on to this new routine.

- Keeping in touch with the customer's needs will become an ongoing fire service challenge. The ability to continually repackage the organization and how we deliver service will directly regulate our survival in a rapidly changing future. Those flexible souls who can continually redefine their jobs ahead of the change curve will grow and prosper. Those who can't, sadly will become roadkill on

Handwritten margin notes:

who has authority? those who have rank.

Bosses empower workers on the task level.

Workers extend respect (empowerment) on the strategic level.

the employment highway — members who staunchly maintain "they hired me to fight fire (only)" will become "sail firefighters" — occupational roadkill that is run over and smushed so flat they can be recreationally sailed like a frisbee. Successful fire service redefinition will be the result of connecting customer needs with smart, agile organizations who are seeking opportunities to serve those needs. Simply, we must move quickly and smartly to always keep the customer in the center of the organizational bull's-eye. Developing the inclination and ability to manage a moving organizational bulls-eye will become the exciting definition of future fire service success.

We must continually
improve our customer
service performance.

8.
We must continually improve our customer service performance.

This little paper has presented a pretty good slug of customer service ideas and maybe a vision or two. What most of this really means is that we must keep our organization moving and changing to match the needs of our customers and our department members. The current fire service environment has lots of positive and some scary challenges and opportunities. We must package up our organization to somehow effectively fit into that environment.

We should approach the future with a great deal of optimism. Our history reflects we can do about anything that is required to reach our objective — we practice this in the street (where we should really keep score) every day. We do this basically because of the dedication, brains, fortitude, and good nature of our firefighters. Sometimes, the American fire service beats itself up by a self-characterization of being backward, inbred, and resisting change. This is baloney — while firefighters are naturally skeptical, not easily impressed, and don't change just for the sake of change,  we are not going to hell in a hand basket or a 1500 GPM pumper. Our customers will love us for the next 200 years for the same reasons they have for the last 200. We are there when they need us, we care about them, we get the job done, and they can trust us (WOW!).

What we are about now is making a good thing even better, gently overpowering and bringing along the negative people and stuff in our business, and always redirecting ourselves in a positive direction.

While everything is not perfect and never will be, I'm sure happy we didn't seek employment in the savings & loan business, the U.S. Senate, or as a television evangelist. We must continually improve our approach to the management of change to prepare us for what is next. We must recognize that customer change must drive effective fire service change in the future.

I dug out my most recent notes on change and came up with the following blivets:

- Expect change (don't be surprised).
- Regard change as a process, not an event.
- The past no longer predicts the future (like it did in the past).
- The future will arrive sooner than we think.
- The future will not be what we expect.
- Currently, most fire-service change is driven by crisis.
- Traditional (MBO) planning can't keep up.
- Support must now replace old time control.
- Systems are mindsets.
- Don't fall in love with the past.
- It will never be like it was.
- Change will generally beat up the change agents.
- Change agents are tough and will survive.
- Closed systems die.
- Even though we change, there will always be problems.
- They pay us to solve those problems.
- We should always shoot for the best set of problems.
- Very little is sacred anymore — everything is fair game for improvement.
- Success/fun = "Let's try it."
- Effective longevity at all levels = constant retool/renew.
- When you're through changing — you're through.

We must develop a change plan for our own:

- Happiness
- Survival/welfare
- Sanity
- Prosperity/growth

A major function for fire service leaders is to set the stage and then manage the change process. Simply, we can "move the machine" and improve our service delivery capability (or really anything else) only to the extent we can create a steady stream of effective, ongoing change. This capability will determine if we control circumstances, or if circumstances control us. We have a fire service plan for every other blessed thing, so here goes my laundry list of basic organizational pieces that together give us a fighting chance to capture and manage the management process:

- Management by opportunity
- Relationship management
- Continual learning/unlearning/relearning
- Corporate communications

- Organizational geometry and behavior
- Action management
- Respect the past
- Organizational foundations

Management by Opportunity

Most of today's (older) public managers were raised with a management by objective education foundation. This system was based upon and worshipped quality, quantity, time, and cost as the elements managers used to plan, measure, control, and execute organizational outcomes. It was a great system if things were going along in a slow and steady sort of way. It was designed (on purpose) to create predictability, minimize risk, and to eliminate surprises. While some of the traditional MBO pieces will probably always be useful to managers, today the overall, old-time MBO approach is way too slow, incremental, and cumbersome to keep up with changes and to take advantage of our chances to move ahead.

In today's environment, the smart money has changed the O in MBO from objectives to opportunities. This is an important shift in our mentality and approach. When seeking opportunity becomes the basis of our game plan throughout the organization from the fire gods in the puzzle palace to the firefighters in the street, we begin to use our collective energy to improve operations in a way that actually matches current reality.

This is not a nice neat change package — continually foraging for opportunities creates a lot of the confusion, disorder, and new energy that the original MBO system was in place to explicitly control (actually eliminate). This change causes some old roles and some old rules to not apply anymore. Effective leaders must now listen smart from the top; workers must now talk smart from where we actually meet customers up close and personal and can best see and understand their needs. Middle managers must actively and skillfully keep the whole game plan moving and everyone and everything connected. Sometimes this new approach looks a lot like we turned the asylum over to the inmates....because we have. For 200 years, us regal, exalted, fire service managers really thought we had our human resources absolutely under control — and then went home at four-thirty every afternoon. Little did we know, the troops (inmates) had fun, got the job done, and took care of the customers just fine until we got back at eight-thirty the next morning. All the new opportunity-based MBO does is make it official. This approach requires leaders to lead, managers to manage, workers to take responsibility for the work, and for everybody to focus on customer service, listen to each other, help each other, and to put the small stuff in perspective. This new approach actually authorizes workers to have a good time (fun) doing their jobs.

Relationship Management

Basic relationship management plan:

Do whatever is required to create high quality, long-term, lasting, genuine trust, trust, trust, trust, trust, trust, trust, trust, trust, trust, trust,

trust, trust, trust, trust, trust, trust, trust, trust, trust, trust, trust, trust,
trust, trust, trust, trust, trust, trust, trust, trust, trust, trust, trust, trust,
trust, trust, trust, trust, trust, trust, trust, trust, trust, trust, trust, trust,
trust, trust, trust, trust, trust, trust, trust, trust, trust, trust, trust, trust,
trust, trust, trust, trust, trust, trust, trust, trust, trust, trust, trust, trust,
trust, trust, trust, trust, trust, trust, trust, trust, trust, trust, trust, trust,
trust, trust, trust, trust, trust, trust, trust, trust, trust, trust, trust, trust,
trust, trust, trust, trust, trust, trust, trust, trust, trust, trust, trust, trust,
trust, trust, trust, trust, trust.

I asked Kathi to print trust 100 times as a dumb way to make a smart point. Particularly for fire service leaders, we should subliminally substitute a new name for Fire Department and call it what it really is — the Relationship Department (that goes to fires and does a lot of other stuff). We operate in a way that is solely based on relationships — everything we are and everything we do (which is a lot) emerges from functional, effective relationships. The essence and result of relationship(s) is *trust*....plain and simple.

> **It's 4:15 a.m.; Mrs. Smith smells smoke; she calls 911. During the response, the first-due engine company officer obtains the call back number from alarm (next door neighbor) and makes contact with Mrs. Smith from the engine's cellular phone. He indicates their response time and quickly describes what will happen when the company arrives. He tells Mrs. Smith to stay safely next door and someone will make contact with her as quickly as possible. We arrive in 3½ minutes with two engine companies, one ladder company, one rescue company, one support company, and one Battalion Chief. We have the capability to pump 4,500 gallons per minute (good plugs), which could literally fill her house up with water in fifteen minutes if it didn't leak. The ladder company carries the monster tools of destruction and XXXL truckies, who could also literally cut her house off its foundation in the same fifteen minutes. We enter, check on her welfare, and put her in the BC's suburban so that she can call her daughter and tell her she is okay (in case the neighbors call). We get Skippy and Fluffy (mutt & meow) out and secure them. We discover a minor electrical fire behind a plug in her (famous) kitchen that has caused the problem and the smoke. We put down hall runners and throw a salvage cover under the fire area. We carefully open up the wall (with a small drywall saw), check for extension, complete extinguishment, and remove residual water and fire debris. We disconnect the electric supply (trip the circuit breaker) to the area and leave a note for the electrician that describes the problem/our action. We blow residual smoke out of the house, explain to Mrs. Smith what happened, what we did, and what she should do to get her life back to normal (insurance, electrician, etc.). We tuck Skippy, Fluffy, and Mrs. Smith back into bed. We reverse our response, and we do the same.**

> **Two days later, our Department automatically sends Mrs. Smith a customer service evaluation card that asks her to evaluate our performance. She indicates that we were prompt, ef-**

fective, and nice. We distribute her comments to the troops that responded. The Battalion Chief conducts a (routine) coffee-table critique of the event and thanks them for their efforts and positive customer response. The troops suggest that smaller pieces of black plastic would be less cumbersome than their large salvage covers for small local jobs (like Mrs. Smith's) and that a battery-operated saw would be quicker and cleaner than a manual dry wall saw. The BC assigns those who suggested such changes as pilot program managers and coordinates the improvements with the department's logistics staff. The system (bosses) was accessible, open, and supportive of making changes that will improve our performance.

Imagine the power and impact of this event within our world after we re-create it 1,000, 10,000, or a bazillion times. It isn't complicated or mysterious....it is based on a trust-induced relationship.

Exactly the same outcome occurs inside our organization as it does with Mrs. Smith, and there is an internal organizational translation to Mrs. Smith's 4:15 a.m. situation where she wakes up and smells smoke. What happens next is based on how she trusts us and the system. When we wake up at 4:15 a.m. and smell smoke (in effect) inside our department is when major change is occurring. We are scared; we don't know what will happen to us. We are worried about our own survival and welfare, and the survival and welfare of everyone and everything we care about. What happens next is based on how the participants ask and answer two timeless questions we all ask ourselves about our organization and our boss — Can I trust you? — Do you care about me? Imagine if we get the same service as internal customers as Mrs. Smith received as an external customer and the effect it will have on how we feel about each other and change in general. Everything occurs or doesn't occur after trust. Don't ever sacrifice a relationship (trust) for an outcome.

Continual Learning/Unlearning/Relearning

It may be that our old, original fire fighting lessons provide the most practical and understandable direction for managing current fire service change. On the fireground, time is compressed, consequences are 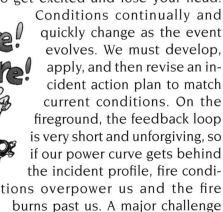 severe, information is generally incomplete and not too accurate. There is a huge temptation to get excited and lose your head. Conditions continually and quickly change as the event evolves. We must develop, apply, and then revise an incident action plan to match current conditions. On the fireground, the feedback loop is very short and unforgiving, so if our power curve gets behind the incident profile, fire conditions overpower us and the fire burns past us. A major challenge is for firefighters to quickly assemble information, act on that information, and then move on to the next operational opportunity. We continually unload old information, receive, process, and act on new information. We must be careful to not fall in love with an old, outdated attack plan that is not working — our response should not be working harder on the wrong plan — it should be to identify and move on to support the opportunities within the new plan. We are operationally effective to the extent we can change quickly enough to always be in the right place, doing the right thing, at the right time.

Today's management conditions closely resemble a fire fighting operation and in the same way requires us to have the ability to learn/unlearn/relearn. The learning/unlearning/relearning process provides the capacity, and over time, develops (in us) the natural inclination and organizational agility to change to match current and forecasted conditions. This is when change becomes a process we expect and not an event that always surprises us.

On the fireground, if we can't learn effectively, the roof comes in on us — today, it works about the same down at the office. How we continually learn from "the roof coming in on us" will pretty much determine our success and survival.

A dynamic piece of this learning process is what actually happens when we go out into the real world and take care of real customers who have real problems. Simply, for us, "customerland" produces the ultimate lessons. One such lesson is that it is virtually impossible to always deliver perfect service and that there is generally a lesson (or two) involved when we don't do it just right. If we are serious about getting better, we must pay attention and capitalize on those local experiences (lessons). They are the most relevant because they involve the actual use of our own local resources. Lessons are not all created equal. Sometimes they come in packages that can be integrated into our ongoing system and produce nice, easygoing incremental changes. Other times, they come flying through the transom and bash us in the head. Particularly in these cases, we better have a system already in place to effect change quickly (that's what this section is all about).

Our local service delivery system is made up of people, hardware, and systems, and those basic system elements have good days and bad days. Sometimes the bad days are a result of human flubs — fatigue, anger, inattention, hearing/seeing difficulties, pride, ego, bad manners, bad decisions, impatience, lousy supervision, temporary burnout, etc. Hardware requires good design, maintenance, and operation. Operational and management systems currently must struggle to stay ahead of rapidly changing service delivery reality. One of the major ways we keep it all working okay is to continually use all of the pieces and parts. When it works good, we reinforce it — when we screw up, we fix it.

Our last customer service story may serve as an example of an experience that produced a major lesson and an opportunity to improve our customer service performance.

This customer service example involves another EMS situation that occurred on an airplane that landed in our town. We became aware of the customer service details of this particu-

lar incident only because one of the passengers who was on the same flight and became directly involved wrote a letter to the Fire Chief. The letter writer is a critical coronary care registered nurse who was a passenger on the flight along with a 65-year-old man who had a serious heart attack about an hour before their scheduled landing. It was pretty easy to see that her letter was not junk mail — it was well stated, perfectly typed on high-class personalized stationery, addressed directly, correctly, and confidentially to the Fire Chief. The nurse lived in the midwest and was travelling home from a medical conference. Early in the letter she described and validated herself as a highly experienced practitioner, a supervisor, and a medical educator. She had so many letters behind her name that it looked like an eye chart.

Luckily (for the medical customer), both the critical care nurse (letter writer) and a cardiologist (M.D.) were passengers on the plane and attended to the man. They were able to stabilize and monitor him during the remainder of the flight. He had suffered a serious attack, so their care was intense and continuous right up to the time the plane pulled up to the arrival gate.

The pilot called air traffic control as soon as he was informed of the medical problem. The flight was then fast-tracked onto our airport. They alerted 911, and we dispatched a paramedic company and an ambulance. The units were waiting when the plane landed. The man was serious enough that the pilot decided to hold the passengers in their seats so that the paramedics could quickly board, do their thing, and remove and transport the customer to a medical facility. The plane lands without incident and gets to the gate okay....so far, so good.

Enter our two young, brave paramedics. Both are well trained, experienced, very capable, cross trained firefighter-medics assigned to a busy downtown unit. They are both in their mid-30s, handsome, athletic, and proudly display their paramedic patches on their snazzy-snug navy blue uniform t-shirts. Both are really good guys, but are susceptible to falling into a trancelike state when they are struck by a self-induced impression of their considerable inherent coolness.

Now our guys make their grand entrance. The flight attendants quickly direct them to the customer. At that point, the critical care nurse attempts to make contact with the medics to give them a basic, standard description of Mr. Smith's airborne coronary adventure and his current condition. The foolish cardiologist also attempts to get involved in the treatment transfer process. At this point, our medics abruptly and aggressively indicate to both the original care givers (middle-aged, informally dressed, probably looking a little rumpled after their high altitude treatment experience) to clear the area so that they can apply their medical magic. The nurse, probably accustomed to routinely dealing with regular (i.e., rational) medical folks, who as a standard process effectively communicate and connect during the transfer of medical command and treatment, gives it another shot. Our guys are now on a roll and they don't get any smarter as this operetta plays on. They explain again, with enthusiasm, that they are prepared to forcefully (!) remove any amateur medical interlopers who interfere with their Godlike treatment. At this point, the nurse/doctor team realize that they are dealing with the deranged, so they stand back and observe the paramedic treatment process.

The nurse indicated (with amazing objectivity) that the treatment the medics extended to Mr. Smith after they demonstrated their astronomical interpersonal skills was exceptional. She commended them for their gentle treatment, skillful stabilization, correct medical support, and adept removal from the plane. She related that she trained paramedics and would be proud and happy if her students performed (technically) as well.

The next (and final) paragraph got her back in the swing of describing her feelings. She finished up by saying that she had never been treated as badly as she had been treated by Frick and Frack in her entire life and that she would never (ever) consider coming to our moth eaten town even if we were handing out hundred dollar bills on every street corner. Clearly stating that the Fire Chief has to (also) be a low-grade imbecile to employ such uncivilized cretins provided a strong ending to the letter.

As he finished re-reading the letter, the tired old Fire Chief took a deep breath, decided to expand the letter into a multi-media experience, and dialed up the letter writer on the phone (number on the stationery). The phone rings, the Fire Chief holds his breath, and she answers on about the third ring. She sounds just like she writes: smart, awake, experienced, capable, and tough. The Fire Chief introduces himself, tells her how much he enjoyed reading her letter (as opposed to falling into a fully involved basement), and asks if they could discuss what happened. She thanks him for calling and basically restates the story, with added emphasis and emotional detail. The Fire Chief listens patiently, grunts and uhmm uhmms to let her know that he is still hanging on the other end. When she runs down, the Fire Chief indicates that he will initiate an investigation and will get back to her. She thanks him again for the call and restates how important she believes high quality medical care is. She also says that failing to effectively transfer the patient through the pre-hospital food chain puts that person at a treatment disadvantage (and isn't nice). The Fire Chief agrees, they say goodbye and hang up.

The Fire Chief asks administrative staff to dig the details of the call out of our incident response records. They investigate and indicate that indeed we received such a request for service at the airport on the day and at the time the nurse indicated in her letter. The records also reflect that we treated and then transported a 65-year-old man to the closest hospital. Staff checks with the hospital and learns that the customer was treated in the emergency room, transferred to a critical care coronary unit where he resided for three days. He was then moved to a regular medical area and was released seven days after his initial admission. The call actually occurred as the nurse had described — she had not mistaken landing in Albuquerque for landing in Phoenix (darn).

The Fire Chief then shares the epic letter with the chain of command who handled the call and asks the BC to investigate and find out what happened. The BC is given a copy of the letter, so the medics can see exactly what the nurse has stated. The BC visits the medics to get their side of the story. The medics read the letter, are straightforward and forthright. They remember the basics of the call including the man and woman who were tending to Mr. Smith when they got on the plane. They state "yeah, we probably told them to get back and let us achieve our next miracle in modern medicine." The BC asks the medics if they had any conversation with the caregivers. The medics state that they had no idea that they (nurse/doc) had any medical experience, so there was little reason to converse with such amateurs. The BC asks how they could have learned anything about them when they told them both to hit the road. The medics shrug and restate that they had no idea who they were, they looked like average frumpy airline passengers. The medics agree after reading the letter and learning that plain old Jack was a cardiologist and plain old Jill was a critical care nurse, that they probably should have asked them who they were and what treatment they had provided prior to the arrival of our two miracle workers. The BC also suggests that if they had conducted a sensible conversation, the medics could have recorded what airborne treatment was extended, gotten some details about the nurse and the doctor (like maybe a business card), and extended some sort of nice thank-you for stepping in and helping Mr. Smith in his time of need.

As the BC continues the discussion, he becomes concerned about how routine the medic's response and reaction appears and asks "Is this normal procedure for you guys?" They explain that sometimes customers come with folks who are trying to assist them prior to our arrival. In those cases, it may be necessary to quickly clear the area to effectively focus on the medical treatment process — or whatever the incident problem involves. The BC asks if they ever deal in a positive way with those who are already on the scene when they arrive. They respond that their usual approach is to quickly determine the customer's problem and then go to work solving those problems (tunnel vision).

The medics indicate they feel badly for the confusion that their airplane approach has created. They also observe (correctly) that the Department has never developed any formal direction for dealing with those folks who are part of an incident when we arrive. The BC asks them to think about and record what action the Department could take to improve our interaction with the Good Sams we encounter in our service delivery travels. The BC reports up the chain of command that what the nurse described in her conversation with the Fire Chief was essentially correct and that things did happen the way she related.

The Fire Chief thanks the BC for his follow-up and asks him to begin development of an SOP to deal with our on-scene interaction with on-scene incident participants. The BC begins development of such a program and uses the medics to assist. They write the SOP and process it through our regular procedure review process. Once reviewed, the SOP is placed in the regular training system used to implement new Department procedures. The Good Sam SOP is really simple and includes the following checklist:

- Include Good Sams in the initial situation evaluation (size-up).
- Quickly establish positive contact with Good Sams.
- Ask them what has already happened and what has been done to help the customer/situation.
- Check and verify their welfare.
- Find out who they are and if they have any special expertise.
- If you need assistance and they are okay — let them continue helping.
- Don't let them get hurt.
- Be certain to thank them.
- Get details for a commendation, if appropriate.
- Include their personal details and their action in the incident report.

After the BC reports back on his interview with the medics, the Fire Chief calls the nurse back and describes what action has taken place. He indicates to her that her description of the incident was accurate and that our Department made a mistake in how we treated her and the doctor. He apologizes for their actions. He then tells her that her letter triggered the development of a new procedure that will establish a standard approach to positively deal with Good Samaritans. He promises that he will send a copy of the procedure and the implementation plan along as soon as they are ready. She thanks him for the second call and says that she looks forward to the next installment.

When the SOP and the plan are complete, we send them along to her. The nurse writes back and thanks us for our responsiveness to her complaint. She ratchets back some of the feelings about us that she described in her initial letter. In fact, she indicates that she would no longer be pleased if killer bees invaded our city and stung everyone 1000 times (I made the part up about the bees) — actually, she complimented us on how we handled the situation.

Buried in this little scenario is another little laundry list of how we might react to complaints and screwups:

- Do whatever is necessary to stabilize the situation.
- Quickly contact the person who complained.
  - Tell them that you have received their complaint.
  - You are investigating.
  - You will recontact them.
  - Obtain any additional information they have (listen).
- Find out what actually happened.
  - Listen to all participants.
  - Don't be defensive.
  - Don't decide anything until you have heard everyone's story.
- If we screwed up, develop a basic plan.
  - First recover from the event that caused the complaint.
  - Develop a plan that fixes the problem so that it doesn't happen again.
  - Use the regular in-place management/operational system whenever possible to help solve the problem.
- Contact the customer.
  - Tell them we screwed up.
  - Tell them we are sorry (apologize).
  - Determine if we can do something that makes them feel better.
  - Describe the plan to fix the problem.
  - Use the participants (as much as possible) to develop the solution that will prevent the problem from

occurring again — focus on fixing the problem, not assigning blame.

- Many times complaints/screwups create well-disguised opportunities (for clever, crafty managers).

Corporate Communications

During periods of active change (like now), learning and communications are joined at the hip because to be effective they both must be based on current, accurate, relevant information. The ability of the organization to provide such information will become a major element in maintaining the ability to change effectively.

Given our decentralization, shift arrangement, and activity, a fire department can be a strange animal to communicate with. Firefighters have a humongous need for information, and if the organization does not supply it effectively, other more informal ways develop — firefighters become very creative in using these informal networks (to say the least). An absolutely incredible informal information exchange system exists in most fire departments. In many cases, it is impossible for the formal system to beat the informal system.

Our organizational ability to manage official communications in most cases is still fairly unrefined. We must create and then operate a practical, on-line system to effectively assemble, package, and transmit timely, accurate information throughout the organization in the form of a deliberate organizational plan. Every change has an information/communications component that will generally regulate the effectiveness of the new plan. Providing enough information in the beginning of a proposed change makes life easier for everyone involved. This does not occur consistently unless the organization builds a corporate communications system into the regular department management process.

Almost any survey, questionnaire, or inquiry into organizational effectiveness and problems will result in firefighters marking "communications" as the most serious department problem. This can be a reflection of both a substantive difficulty and a personal perception and feeling — change agents must pay attention to both. It probably requires a lot of mechanisms to effectively connect everyone involved with timely, adequate information — written stuff, SOPs, newsletters, memos, bulletins, buckslip weekly info packages, meetings, critiques, personal face-to-face interaction, classes, videotapes, interactive video, cable, satellite department transmissions, carrier pigeons, smoke signals, tom-toms, etc. All this not only exchanges real information, but perhaps even more importantly, gives people in the organization the very personal feeling that the system is anxious, open, and positive about providing enough information to do our jobs effectively and will work hard to do so. It's hard to trust the system and the people who manage it when you feel they are not telling you enough or that they aren't telling you the truth. The system is based upon trusting each other and simply cannot operate unless everyone tells the truth — even when it is painful to do so. Anyone dumb enough to screw around with the truth in an organization like a fire department (very permanent/very long memory) is in for an enormous amount of personal grief. Sooner or later the nontruthful fairy tales always catch up to the teller and generally have some sharp edges that can cause lots of pain. Truth is the same for all people. There isn't a bigger and better truth for Chiefs and another for the Indians. We must keep on communicating until our people feel communicated with. Don't lock up information or ever believe anything is off the record....only idiots and sophomores believe there are really any secrets in a fire department.

Organizational Geometry and Behavior

Old-time fire department organization charts resemble a big, tall, narrow, upside down ice cream cone. The Fire Chief is perched at the top, firefighters are on the very bottom; lots of layers are in between. It reflected what was essentially a military model that was designed to do highly regimented work, control the troops, eliminate disorder, and deliver the mail. The guys on the top told the guys in the middle what to tell the guys on the bottom to do (only guys in those days). The system used rules, ranks, and the chain of command as major management-control mechanisms. It wasn't a bad design if you were fighting a war in 1914, but the design and the mentality that goes with it really sucks when applied to operating a fire department today. It was indeed designed to fight a war with an outside army, and indeed required (and still does) a war to change anything in or about the organization. Another design characteristic is that a customer never showed up anywhere in the chart (actually, the point of the whole military drill was to kill the enemy, not to serve any customer). There are a lot of ideas currently floating around regarding how modern organizations should look — while the design is an important element in effectiveness, it seems the most important part is how the system acts and what that action produces for the customer and the members. The fire service is generally shifting to a flatter, more modern organizational design, but during the transition, the baby should be seat-belted to the tub. Simply, everyone needs to be brought along so that we all arrive together wherever the new design is taking us.

Action Management

Another organizational element that has already been mentioned in several places is an action management model that combines, connects, and integrates the development of SOPs, training, application, critique, and revision. This approach is a basic, straightforward way the organization can decide on the details that relate to the use of resources and assets in a standard situation. This design also provides the basis for training on the SOPs that will actually be used. SOPs then provide the framework for how operations are conducted (Ops manual). After those operations are completed, the SOPs provide the structure for a standard review and critique. Based on the lessons learned and reinforced, an action plan for improvement is developed. Revisions are driven by that plan. The ongoing use of this model becomes a powerful mechanism to get good and stay good.

A logical development in improving customer service (or anything else) is to plug it into this model. Good service isn't voodoo, and lends itself as much to the application of the action model as any traditional tactical activity (like laying hose and raising ladders). The action model is a practical way to translate a good idea in someone's head to an effective service delivery operation that actually occurs in the street. The ongoing application of this model (and approach) begins to change how we feel about it being possible to improve our operations because we have a very simple (actually routine), safe, effective way to do it. The system also becomes the "entry point" for us to begin to manage not only performance but also attitudes about service delivery. In fact, the quickest and most effective way to change our members' attitudes is to first consistently change their behavior. The most effective way to send a really believable message (as an example) to our troops about customer service is to write a salvage box SOP, train everyone how to use it, provide the boxes on the rigs, and integrate loading up the stuff Mrs. Smith loves when she has her fire into the regular incident management system. After the troops go through this routine, hug and kiss them and buy them ice cream. This feels good and makes them want to do it again (and again). This is a natural approach and the next logical step in improving the service we extend to both our internal and external customers.

Respect the Past

Continued improvement necessarily involves changes that occur at what is (in effect) the end of a series of ongoing efforts, events, projects, and organizational investments that got us where we are today. This series of activities forms a history that reflects a cast of organizational characters who have been involved up to our current stage of development. This history and those characters not only describe the past, they also set the stage for the future. These players have an interest, a stake, and a certain predictable affection for what it took to develop, defend, learn, and apply all the pieces of what are (now) in place. These old soldiers have the scars that become the trophies that validate them as players who have earned their colors. We all move through our departments with about the same glacial speed, so in most cases, many of these former program players are still hanging around in the organization. They have a certain built-in influence (i.e., control) over the formal and informal process(es) that regulate how (and sometimes if) changes occur.

Many times, the latest change agent shows up in the "middle of the movie" as a savior "riding a white horse." These characters can be directed by a preoccupation (tunnel vision) on how the change will improve the future. Problems occur when such agents of a brighter tomorrow (typically smart/energetic/aggressive/empowered) look only forward and fail to balance the future with the past. What this balance requires is for the change agent to look more like a quiet person who is dealing with the next logical change — and skip the white horse routine. That person can then naturally also look backward to acknowledge the past efforts that form the foundation for the next set of improvements. This approach makes the past more, not less, valuable. All of our lives would become a lot easier if we added this standard balancing step in the change process....it's pretty easy to do a basic history check to see who has an emotional, psychic, or nostalgic feeling about the program, activity, or thing we are currently fooling with. We can then acknowledge, celebrate, and thank the participants for what has been done up until now. Showing more genuine respect for the past would also create a regular internal process where organizational improvements naturally and continually emerge out of effective past efforts. Those who were involved in the past program development become the respected and recognized program ancestors. It also makes a lot of sense and creates a more effective level of continuity to wherever possible involve and include past program players in new program changes.

1985 AWARD FOR BEST UNIFORM DESIGN

Another benefit of this approach is that everyone in the organization might be more conditioned and prepared to plan for and expect continued change as a regular and positive organizational process. Simply, such regular change is how things keep getting better. Documenting the details of development would create a valuable description of how and why the organization looks as it does — this documentation becomes, in effect, "writing on the walls of the caves." It then becomes an important tribal ritual for the members to read those "walls" to develop a more effective perspective of how they fit into and become a part of that writing (history). Our family-oriented structure and mentality inherently have a variety of very powerful ways to cause respect and loyalty mistakes to be very expensive and painful. Effectively connecting our past, present, and future is a big time element in making us all happier and healthier customers in and around the change process. Successful, long-term change management requires that we are not paralyzed by the past or terrorized by the future.

Organizational Foundations

....And finally (whew), how in the world do we survive all this gut-wrenching, bone-crushing change? How do we get through every new management craze? How do we react every time the Fire Chief awakes from a trance and sees a new vision? The way we keep going is by relating and returning to the foundations of our organization. They are the basis of what we really are and what we will always be. We don't talk a lot about them, and I won't either. These are the ones I'm not ready to change:

- Firefighters look out for each other — we will put our welfare on the line to protect and save each other.
- Firefighters stick together.
- We go in together; we come out together.
- Being a firefighter is a lifetime deal.
- We prove ourselves by executing in difficult situations.
- We help our friends; we will defend ourselves against our adversaries — we have a long memory of both groups.
- Loyalty is the glue that holds us together.
- We will not leave our wounded or dead behind.
- We all wear the same uniform (colors) — in the Phoenix Fire Department we are all blue.

We must continually improve our customer service performance.

- Firefighters must earn the right to belong.
- People trust firefighters.
- We are heros to kids.
- Firefighters make and keep a promise to protect the customer.
- Customer service will always be human being to human being.
- Everything is passed on — we are an old, continuous, long-term service; our ancestors set the stage for us; we are now setting the stage for the next generation.
- We have inside language, rituals, ceremonies, rites of initiation, acceptance, passage, and exit.
- We have our own warped, twisted sense of humor.
- The past gives us our identity, the future gives us our purpose — we must respect both.
- We will embrace positive change to remain effective.
- Fire is still our middle name and always should be.
- God meant fire trucks to always be red.

Appendix A

NOT ON TEST →

Personnel	**PHOENIX FIRE DEPARTMENT ADMINISTRATIVE REGULATIONS**
RECORDS OF EXCEPTIONAL PERFORMANCE (GREEN SHEETS)	M.P. 105.05A 6/94-R Page 1 of 2

PURPOSE

The purpose of this procedure is to establish an additional method for the Fire Department members to be recognized for exceptional performance. This procedure will guide Phoenix Fire Department supervisors in dealing with exceptional performance by using the Record of Exceptional Performance (Green Sheet) to document the incident. If supervisors have any questions concerning exceptional performance, they should be directed to the Department Personnel section.

POLICY

It is the policy of the Phoenix Fire Department to appropriately recognize members of the Department for exceptional performance.

Green Sheets may be presented to any member of the Fire Department, a person active in the Department Cadet program, or a citizen in active volunteer service.

There is no limit placed on the number of Green Sheets any individual may be awarded.

RECOMMENDATIONS FOR GREEN SHEETS

Any supervisor of the Department may recommend a member for a Record of Exceptional Performance (Green Sheet). The recommendation should be made to the member's immediate supervisor via telephone or written documentation. The member's supervisor will acknowledge receipt of the written recommendation if requested by the sender.

PRESENTATION OF GREEN SHEETS

Green Sheets will be presented to the member(s) by the immediate supervisor at an appropriate time. The original will be forwarded through proper channels to be placed into the member's personnel file. A copy will be given to the member and another copy is to be forwarded to the Fire Chief.

Personnel	PHOENIX FIRE DEPARTMENT ADMINISTRATIVE REGULATIONS
RECORDS OF EXCEPTIONAL PERFORMANCE (GREEN SHEETS)	M.P. 105.05A 6/94-R Page 2 of 2

ROUTING AND RETENTION

The immediate supervisor will forward the original copy to the District Commander or Section Head for review. The District Commander or Section Head will forward the original copy to the Personnel Services Division to be placed into the employee's personnel file for the duration of employment.

FIRE DEPARTMENT
RECORD OF EXCEPTIONAL PERFORMANCE

1. Employee	2. Division/Section
3. Classification	4. Date prepared

5. Initiator of commendation, if other than supervisor

6. Description and date of exceptional performance

7. Supervisor's comments and date of presentation

8. Employee's comments

9. Supervisor's signature	10. Employee's signture

Original: Personnel file   90-01D New 8/89
Copy: Employee
          Fire Chief

Sectors	**PHOENIX FIRE DEPARTMENT**
	STANDARD OPERATING PROCEDURES
	M.P. 214.01C
OCCUPANT SERVICES SECTOR	05/95-R Page 1 of 3

The purpose of this procedure is to establish the role and responsibilities of the Occupant Services Sector.

The Occupant Services Sector shall be established by the Incident Commander at all working structure fires, and as early in the incident as is practical. The Occupant Services Sector should also be established at any incident where the need is identified; Fire, EMS, Special Operations, etc.

The Occupant Services Sector is a critical extension of our service delivery, and serves as the liaison between the Fire Department and those citizens (responsible parties) directly, or perhaps indirectly involved in or affected by the incident.

If necessary, Command will request additional resource in order to establish the Occupant Services Sector. An additional engine, ladder, or battalion chief is acceptable. If necessary, at prolonged incidents, in order to return fire companies and personnel to service, Command may assign staff personnel to this function. The Occupant Services Sector responsibilities may extend beyond the termination of the incident.

RESPONSIBILITIES:

The Occupant Services Sector should consider offering the following services to the occupant/responsible parties. It should be noted that other occupant service needs may be identified and should be addressed as part of the Department's customer service goals.

- Carry out responsibilities under supervision of loss control officer.

- Explain what happened, what we are doing and why, how long we expect to take until the incident is under control.

- Obtain from occupant/responsible party, any significant information regarding the structure and/or its contents that might assist Command tactically with the operation. Inform Command of this information.

- Provide cellular telephone access.

- Communicate the location to which evacuees have been sent. (Notify the Investigations Sector of this location also when passing on this information.)

- Identify any mental health needs of the occupants/responsible party, as well as any spectators or evacuees. (i.e., affects of shootings, mass casualty, highly visible critical rescue, etc.)

	PHOENIX FIRE DEPARTMENT
Sectors	**STANDARD OPERATING PROCEDURES** M.P. 214.01C
OCCUPANT SERVICES SECTOR	05/95-R Page 2 of 3

- Notify Red Cross, Salvation Army, or other relief agencies.

- Notify other necessary agencies and/or individuals.

- Provide coordination of salvage efforts with the loss control officer.

- Where safe to do so, and after approval from Investigations Sector, coordinate a "Walk-Thru" of the structure with the responsible party.

- Determine the location of valuables in the structure and notify Command/loss control officer.

- Work with loss control and proper utility services to restore power, gas and water, as quickly as possible to reduce additional losses through a loss of business to affected occupants.

- Provide use of service vans as necessary.

- Coordinate site security.
    Fire watch
    Private security company
    Necessary insurance services
    Any services identified as necessary and possible

- Handout and explain the "After the Fire" brochure.

- Assist the occupant in notifying insurance agents, security services, restoration company, etc.

- Provide blankets, and a shelter, where practical to do so, (i.e. and apparatus cab, neighbor's house, etc.) to get occupants out of the weather and at a <u>single</u> location.

- Provide on-going service and support until the customer indicates our services are no longer needed.

- The Occupant Services Sector shall report to Command unless a loss control Branch/Section is assigned, at which time he/she shall report to the loss control officer.

MENTAL HEALTH NEEDS

Occasionally, the public is witness to a critical life-threatening event that can have substantial psychological impacts on them. These persons may be survivors of a critical event or a witness to a mass casualty, or a parent of a severely injured child, or a witness to the death of a family member, etc.

Sectors **OCCUPANT SERVICES SECTOR**	**PHOENIX FIRE DEPARTMENT** **STANDARD OPERATING PROCEDURES** M.P. 214.01C 05/95-R Page 3 of 3

Additionally, witnesses may have misunderstandings of fire department operations that cause a delay in removal of the patient (i.e. trench collapse, an electrocution rescue that is delayed due to energized contact, etc.). Addressing these issues early, on-site, or as soon as possible following the event, can minimize these misunderstandings, and reduce psychological effects, and produce improved relations with the public.

The Occupant Services Sector should consider additional help for these needs. Assistance and advice on availability of mental health services can be obtained through the department's Critical Incident Debriefing Team, the Employee Assistance Program Contractor, the American Red Cross, and in some cases, through the victim's personal medical insurance. Support from the Fire Department Chaplain (CAR810) or local clergy may also be available.

AMERICAN RED CROSS SERVICES

For residential fires where the occupant has suffered a loss of living quarters and clothing, the American Red Cross may be used to provide support.

The American Red Cross can provide some clothing, food, toiletries, and arrange for temporary shelter/housing for the occupants. When contacting the Red Cross, provide the following information:

- Address of the incident.
- Address where victims can be contacted.
- Phone number of contact location.
- Number of displaced persons with information on age, sex, etc.
- Fire Department Incident No.

	PHOENIX FIRE DEPARTMENT
Policy and Procedures	**STANDARD OPERATING PROCEDURES**
	M.P. 214.01F
HANDLING PETS AND OTHER ANIMALS	05/95-R Page 1 of 4

OBJECTIVE

The objective of this procedure is to provide field personnel with guidance in handling pets and other animals that are encountered as a result of an EMS, fire, or other response. These pets or animals may require medical attention and the RP is unknown or unable to care for the animal, or the animal presents a danger to the general public. The pets or animals we encounter might also be trapped or injured.

The pets that we encounter are oftentimes considered by the owners a part of the family. While our primary mission is for the protection and care of the people, we should attempt to provide some level of care to animals in distress whenever feasible and safe to do so as a part of our commitment to customer service. We should display an open, caring concern for pets and animals when we deal with the public in these types of situations.

SAFETY CONSIDERATIONS

Caution should be used in approaching any animal, especially one that is injured. At no time is the safety of our members or that of the public to be compromised by attempting to capture an animal. If there is any doubt, contact one of the agencies listed in this procedure and request that they respond. When dealing with pet or animal rescues, they should be handled similar to "property" when evaluating the risk/gain profile of the incident.

HANDLING PETS

Rescue Efforts (fires, trapped or injured pets)

Rescuing pets or animals during an incident should take the same priority as any loss control activity. An evaluation should be made in terms of the risk or exposure that our personnel would face, versus the likelihood of a positive outcome.

Treatment of Injuries

Animal injuries can be treated in a similar manner as BLS injuries to a human. For example, bleeding can be controlled by direct pressure, elevation, and bandaging. Burns can be cooled with water. Oxygen can be administered for breathing difficulties. Broken limbs can be stabilized using splints. At no time, however, should any attempt be made to provide fluids intravenously.

	PHOENIX FIRE DEPARTMENT
Policy and Procedures	**STANDARD OPERATING PROCEDURES**
	M.P. 214.01F
HANDLING PETS AND OTHER ANIMALS	05/95-R Page 2 of 4

Caring Attitude/Empathy

We should realize that to many people, an animal or pet is considered a family member. We should attempt to treat their concerns with empathy and demonstrate a caring attitude toward their concern. In addition, if the incident has resulted in the death of an animal, we should attempt to assist them in the disposal of the animal by contacting the proper agency, such as the Humane Society or the ASPCA for guidance.

If there is any question regarding the handling or care of a pet, any of the agencies listed in CAD are more than willing to provide guidance and assistance. They all stated that if they are not able to help, they will put us in touch with the proper agency. A case in point may be in the situation where we have treated and transported a rider who has fallen from a horse — what do we do with the horse? The proper agency in this case is Arizona Livestock, but ASPCA stated that they may be able to provide assistance in securing the animal until further action can be taken.

CONTACT NUMBERS

Whenever there is any question regarding handling an injured, non-injured, stray or trapped animal, both the Humane Society and the AZ Society for the Prevention of Cruelty to Animals are willing to either provide direct assistance, or serve as a clearing house in directing us to the proper agency or veterinary service. Both have 24-hour hotlines listed in CAD. To access this information by MDT, type MDTINFO ANIMALS.

Stray animals

For stray, uninjured animals, the call should be referred to the Maricopa County Animal Control (for the telephone number, see "MDTINFO ANIMALS" in the CAD system).

Injured animals

The two primary agencies that can be contacted to respond to injured animal calls (where the animal is not a threat to human safety) are:

> Humane Society
> AZ Society for the Prevention of Cruelty to Animals
> (both numbers are in CAD under "MDTINFO ANIMALS")

	PHOENIX FIRE DEPARTMENT
Policy and Procedures	**STANDARD OPERATING PROCEDURES**
	M.P. 214.01F
HANDLING PETS AND OTHER ANIMALS	05/95-R Page 3 of 4

Both agencies have personnel available 24 hours a day and will respond valley-wide when requested. In the event that they are not able to handle the particular animal involved (for example, an exotic animal), they will provide you with the proper agency to contact for assistance.

If it is necessary to move an injured animal out of a roadway, the recommended procedure it to wrap the animal in a blanket and immobilize it before moving it. Muzzling the animal with material such as kling or a PackStrap would be suggested. This will help to minimize the danger to the rescuers.

Animal Rescue (non-emergency)

In the event that you should encounter an animal that is in distress, but is not injured (cat-in-tree type of call, contact the following agencies (the telephone numbers are in CAD under "MDTINFO ANIMALS"):

> Humane Society
> AZ Society for the Prevention of Cruelty to Animals

If they are unable to provide timely assistance, they will direct you to an agency that can help.

Dangerous Animals

When there is a danger to human safety, Animal Control will respond. (Also request that PD respond.) Their telephone number can be accessed on the CAD via "MDTINFO ANIMALS." Responders should take actions to ensure that the safety of the public and Department members is not compromised while waiting for the arrival of Animal Control.

Immediate actions to be taken if the animal's life is in danger

If an animal is injured to such an extent that its life is in danger, at the discretion of the ranking fire department officer, the animal may be transported to a veterinarian for emergency care. There is a list of emergency animal clinics listed in the CAD under "MDTINFO ANIMALS." The cost for this treatment will either be passed on to the owner, or if the owner cannot be identified, then ASPCA will pay for the treatment. No cost will be incurred by the Fire Department or a member for bringing in an injured animal encountered as part of a fire or EMS response.

The animal should be transported only to those clinics listed. They are equipped with full emergency care facilities and have agreed to accept animals transported by the Fire Department to their facilities.

Policy and Procedures	**PHOENIX FIRE DEPARTMENT**
	STANDARD OPERATING PROCEDURES
HANDLING PETS AND OTHER ANIMALS	M.P. 214.01F 05/95-R Page 4 of 4

It is very important to remember that an injured animal may present a danger to rescuers. At no time should a member's safety be compromised in handling an injured animal. If an animal is considered dangerous, the call should be referred to Maricopa County Animal Control.

<u>Other Agencies</u>

There are other agencies that can respond and deal with injured animals. They are listed under "MDTINFO ANIMALS" in the CAD system. The first call, however, should be either the Humane Society or ASPCA since they have personnel available 24 hours. If they are not able to handle the problem, they will refer you to the appropriate agency.

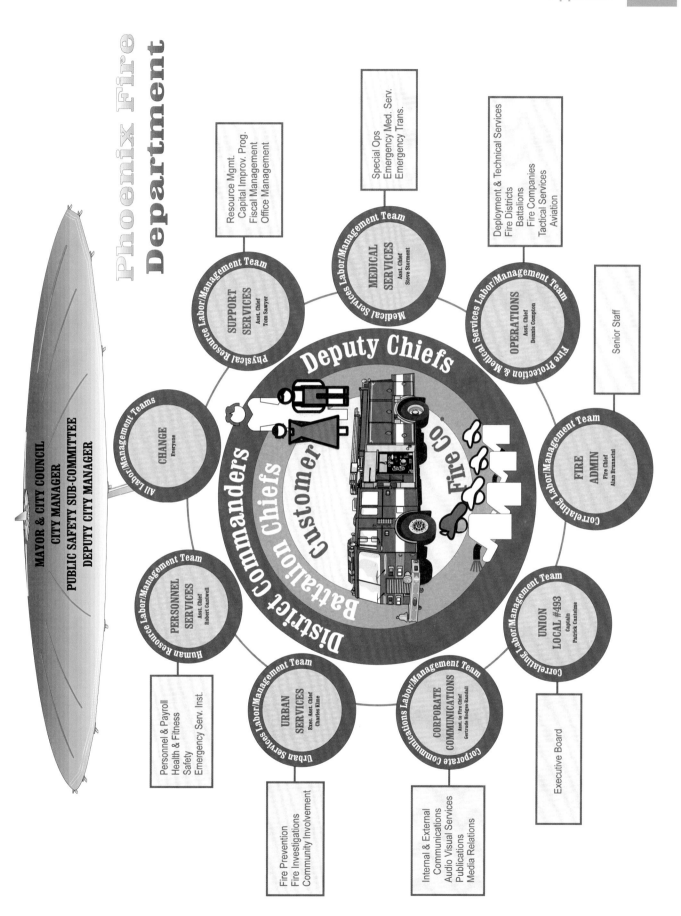

Phoenix Fire Department

MAYOR & CITY COUNCIL
CITY MANAGER
PUBLIC SAFETY SUB-COMMITTEE
DEPUTY CITY MANAGER

CHANGE
Everyone
All Labor/Management Teams

SUPPORT SERVICES
Asst. Chief Tom Sawyer
Physical Resource Labor/Management Team
- Resource Mgmt.
- Capital Improv. Prog.
- Fiscal Management
- Office Management

MEDICAL SERVICES
Asst. Chief Steve Storment
Medical Services Labor/Management Team
- Special Ops
- Emergency Med. Serv.
- Emergency Trans.

OPERATIONS
Asst. Chief Dennis Compton
Fire Protection & Medical Services Labor/Management Team
- Deployment & Technical Services
- Fire Districts
- Battalions
- Fire Companies
- Tactical Services
- Aviation

Senior Staff

FIRE ADMIN
Fire Chief Alan Brunacini
Correlating Labor/Management Team

UNION LOCAL #493
Captain Patrick Cantelme
Correlating Labor/Management Team
Executive Board

CORPORATE COMMUNICATIONS
Asst. to Fire Chief Gertrude Hodges-Randall
Corporate Communications Labor/Management Team
- Internal & External Communications
- Audio Visual Services
- Publications
- Media Relations

URBAN SERVICES
Exec. Asst. Chief Charles Kime
Urban Services Labor/Management Team
- Fire Prevention
- Fire Investigations
- Community Involvement

PERSONNEL SERVICES
Asst. Chief Robert Cantwell
Human Resource Labor/Management Team
- Personnel & Payroll
- Health & Fitness
- Safety
- Emergency Serv. Inst.

Deputy Chiefs
District Commanders
Battalion Chiefs
Customer
Fire Co